BRUMBACK LIBRARY
Dick Tracy :
741.5 DIC
NF   c2

3 3045 00019 2704

741.5   903477
DIC

Dick Tracy   14.95

RW

THE BRUMBACK LIBRARY
OF VAN WERT COUNTY
VAN WERT, OHIO

V-14
588/w

DICK TRACY
America's Most Famous Detective

Edited by Bill Crouch, Jr.

A Citadel Press Book
Published by Carol Publishing Group

741.5
DIC

This book is dedicated to the memory of Chester Gould, Rick Fletcher and John Locher.

Dick Tracy : America's most famous detective / edited by Bill Crouch, Jr.
   p. cm.
ISBN 0-8065-1059-5: $14.95
   1. Dick Tracy (Comic strip)   2. Gould,Chester. I. Crouch, Bill,
1945-
PN6728.D53D53   1987
741.5'0973-dc 19   87-27624
                  CIP

First Carol Publishing Group Edition 1990

Dick Tracy is a registered trademark of Tribune Media Services, Inc.
All Dick Tracy artwork is copyright © Tribune Media Services, Inc. 1987.

"Death in the City" is copyright © Maurice Horn 1987.
"The Aesthetics of Dick Tracy" is copyright © Richard Marschall 1987.
The balance of the text in *Dick Tracy*: *America's Most Famous Detective* is
copyright © Bill Crouch Jr., 1987.

A Citadel Press Book
Published by Carol Publishing Group

Editorial Offices
600 Madison Avenue
New York, NY 10022

Sales & Distribution Offices
120 Enterprise Avenue
Secaucus, NJ 07094

In Canada: Musson Book Company
A division of General Publishing Co. Limited
Don Mills, Ontario

All rights reserved. No part of this book
may be reproduced in any form, except by
a newspaper or magazine reviewer who wishes
to quote brief passages in connection with a review.

Queries regarding rights and permissions
should be addressed to: Carol Publishing Group,
600 Madison Avenue, New York, NY 10022

Manufactured in the United States of America

10 9 8 7 6 5 4 3 2 1

Contents

Introduction 5

"The American Comic Strip Has Sold More Newspapers
Than Any Other Feature in American Journalism," by
Chester Gould 7

Dick Tracy: A Comic Strip Phenomenon 9

Dick Tracy and I, by Chester Gould 37

Death in the City, by Maurice Horn 56

"The Sleet Story: Sam Catchem's First Appearance" 60

The Aesthetics of Dick Tracy, by Richard Marschall 104

Tracy's 25th Anniversary, by Charles Collins 111

A Double Reuben Man: Chester Gould and the National
Cartoonists Society 115

Celebrated Cases 119

"The Governor: Too Soon Old and Too Late Smart" 129

Dick Tracy's Family 144

Rick Fletcher: The Artist Who Carried on the Tracy
Tradition 148

Max Allan Collins: Only the Second Person to Write Dick
Tracy 158

"The Return of Haf-and-Haf," by Fletcher and Collins 165

A Rogues' Gallery Reunion: Tracy's 50th Anniversary 194

Dick Locher: Tracy's Pulitzer Prize Winning Artist 198

"You're in Good Hands with Uppward Lee-Mobile," by
Locher and Collins 206

Tracy Goes to Hollywood 234

Proper Police Procedures 242

Tracy's High-Tech Arsenal 244

Origins of the Wrist Radio 246

The Origin of the Two-Way Wrist TV 252

The Origin of the Two-Way Wrist Computer 254

903477

Introduction

There is no doubt that Dick Tracy is America's most famous detective, and after Sherlock Holmes, the second most famous detective in the world. However, until now an overview of this landmark comic strip has never been published.

Researching and editing *Dick Tracy: America's Most Famous Detective* has been a team effort involving people from different regions of the U.S.A. I would like to thank them for their help, encouragement and co-operation by region. The northeast is the home of the world's paramount Dick Tracy fan and collector, Matt Masterson, without whose resources and wizardry in pasting up reproductions there would be no book. Also thanks to Brice Diedrick, Maurice Horn, Richard Marschall, John Wren, and my editor Allan J. Wilson.

In the midwest, Dick Tracy's home turf, I would like to thank Max Allan Collins, Mrs. Chester Gould, Dick Locher, Jean Gould O'Connell, and Rich Pietrzyk. And for showing me what southern hospitality is all about, I'd like to thank Floridians Jim Cavett and Scott Olsen of Tribune Media Services.

It is my hope that *Dick Tracy: America's Most Famous Detective* will introduce you to the people who have worked on the strip, and show you why Dick Tracy is the most popular detective comic strip in the world.

BILL CROUCH JR.

A special drawing by Chester Gould denotes the end of the New York City newspaper strike of the mid-1960's. The evil Mr. Bribery joins Tracy, Moon Maid, Honeymoon and Junior Tracy in welcoming their readers back.

"The American comic strip has sold more newspapers than any other feature in American journalism."

A personal statement by Chester Gould, creator of Dick Tracy, based on his remarks to the Newspaper Comics Council, November 2, 1972

Not too long ago it was fashionable with some newspaper novices to ask: "What's wrong with the comics?" Well, it's like this: What was wrong with the comics was the guy who kept asking "What's wrong with the comics?"

In many cases this was the same individual who put his comics in little "coffins," $2\frac{1}{4} \times 7\frac{1}{4}$ inches, and buried them alive on page 43 next to the want-ads—and then had the nerve to ask "What's wrong with the comics?" I've seen as many as 22 on one page!

Suppose his front page, which he so lovingly puts together against all the odds set up by television, were reduced to $2\frac{1}{4} \times 7\frac{1}{4}$—and run on page 43 next to the want-ads. How much readership do you think it would get? In my opinion, it would get scarcely one one-hundredth the readership a good comic strip gets under the same handicap.

But to start at the beginning, the comic strip was born in the newspaper office. It is the legitimate child of the newspaper and the only feature today that television has not been able to kidnap from newspapers. TV has sports, news, beauty hints, sex, fashions, problems of the heart, and financial news—but the multi-panel comic strip is still the sole property of newspapers.

And what do a few editors do about it? They say, "Get that little lowbrow bastard out of my way and lock him in the basement!"

The good newspaper appeals to the masses, not just to any particular stratum. Patterson, McCormick, Hearst and other great newsmen knew and practiced this. And appealing to the masses means understanding the man on the street.

It was once pointed out to me that *The New York Times* carries no comic strips and still is a great newspaper. My answer to that was "Think how much greater it could have been *had it carried comic strips.* It might have attained a circulation almost as great as the New York *Daily News*!"

As to the selling of comic strips, I feel there is much to be desired. An important syndicate man recently said to me, "When an editor says 'I don't want that strip anymore,' what can I do?" Well, if the strip is a grabber in the judgment of the salesman, there's a tool he could use. It's called *salesmanship.* Yes, salesmanship. Remember? You present facts, use logic, reason and persuasion. Ford, General Motors, RCA, Zenith, etc., still use it with a great deal of success, wouldn't you agree?

Salesmanship implies *keeping* the product sold, also. In the case of comics, it could be used to induce editors to disinter the little comics from their prison cells and to promote them, even to the use of one on the bottom of the front page. Readers' favorite strips could be used a week at a time on a repeat basis. Any editor who thinks enough of a strip to buy it and give it space—albeit small space— should be willing to back up his judgment.

Now, what does this mean in dollars and cents? Believe me, comics advertising dollars would be a lot easier to come by if individual newspapers publicized and promoted their comics. *Who wants to spend ad dollars with outcasts who, during the week, are locked in tiny cells like drunks?*

Let's face it: You can't ask the elite with the bucks to spend to join your club if you give the impression you're ashamed of the membership!

Also it seems to me that the cozy little group meetings, where everybody engages in repetitive platitudes and listens to critics who lack true understanding of mass newspaper circulation, do not attack the root of the problem. That root is the editor and/or publisher who must be sold on promoting the comics he uses. He must be

shown how this will restore prestige to the product and dollars to his advertising till. This is the big job to be done.

I have been drawing and writing Dick Tracy for 41 years. And the Lord willing, I want to go another 41 years. I'm in excellent health and I'm loaded with experience and the joy of doing my job. I consider myself a newsboy. The sole purpose of a comic strip is to sell newspapers; that makes me a newsboy. The American comic strip is responsible for and has sold more newspapers since its creation than any other feature in American journalism, and I'm proud to be part of it.

We have a heritage of the most precious thing ever developed in the good old U.S.A.—the American newspaper and its comic strips. Let's get out and go with them!

Thank you.

CHESTER GOULD

SEPT. 5 - '68

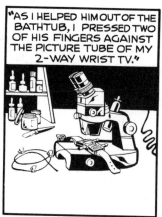

Gathering evidence, in this case a fingerprint, is one of the basic techniques Tracy has used over the years.

Dick Tracy: A Comic Strip Phenomenon

Chester Gould was a man of strong personal convictions. He had an unswervable belief that he would become a famous cartoonist, that he would top his competition in the syndicated cartoon field, that he was in the entertainment business, and that his job was to sell newspapers. All of this molded his creation, "Dick Tracy," into a 20th-century popular culture icon.

In all his years, Chester Gould never faltered or changed his vision of the personal goals he had set for himself as a child in Pawnee, Oklahoma.

The appeal of Dick Tracy is multi-faceted and goes back to the time before television and video cassette recorders. Radio was still the "new" mass medium. The newspaper was the leading means of informing and entertaining the masses.

National syndication of comic strips gave the funnies a national character. "The Gumps," for example, were known from coast to coast. The same held true for "Maggie and Jiggs," "Little Orphan Annie," "Buster Brown," and other comic strips. In 1931, when Dick Tracy was syndicated, America was a far different country from what it is today. College was not an aspiration of most Americans. Major world or national news still brought out newsboys hollaring, "Extra, extra, read all about it!" The Depression had hit America hard. But World War II, the cold war, the bomb, Viet-

nam, and drugs had yet to have their impact on America.

Two key factors in the initial success of the Dick Tracy strip were that it presented something new in the evolution of syndicated comics—realistic violence; and it had the personal support of Captain Joseph Medill Patterson, grandson of the founder of the Chicago *Tribune*, and himself cofounder and director of the New York *Daily News*.

It was Captain Patterson's gift that he could sense the pulse of the American public's desires in mass entertainment. He had been an innovative editor on the family newspaper, the Chicago *Tribune*. His background was private schools, including Groton and Yale, and he had the spirit of an adventurer. Even before graduating from Yale he had spent a year in Asia reporting on the Boxer Rebellion. He later served in the U.S. Army on the Mexican border and then was an artillery officer in World War I in France.

Following World War I, Patterson and his cousin, Colonel Robert Rutherford McCormick, saw an opportunity in founding a mass circulation tabloid newspaper in New York based in the format of the popular tabloid papers in London. *The Illustrated Daily News* was founded. It is now known as the New York *Daily News*.

An analysis made by Coulton Waugh in

A lead-off strip that was used whenever Dick Tracy was published in a new client paper.

his pioneering work of cartoon history, *The Comics* (Macmillan, 1947), holds true today. He noted that Patterson selected strips that featured ordinary people. For example, Dick Tracy was just a young fellow of modest means, and the father of his fiancée Tess Trueheart owned a delicatessen and lived with his family in an apartment over the store. This was hardly an upper-class scenario.

Patterson's cartoon cavalcade had been one of the most enduring in all the history of syndicated comic strips. The strips (with beginning date of publication and type of appeal as analyzed by Coulton Waugh) were: The Gumps (1917), gossip and a realistic family strip; Harold Teen (1919), youth; Gasoline Alley (1919), life itself as the characters in the strip age; Winnie Winkle (1920), "liberated" woman; Smitty (1922), cute kid-stuff; Moon Mullins (1923), burly laughter; Little Orphan Annie (1924), sentiment and survival; Dick Tracy (1931), adventure and fascination with the bizarre, morbid and criminal; Smilin' Jack (1933), flying and sex; and Terry and the Pirates (1934), adventure of a modern sophisticated type.

If, as Chester Gould always maintained, the purpose of the comics is to sell newspapers, Patterson had the Midas touch. The *Daily News's* circulation became the largest of any American newspaper. Gould was always extremely proud that Dick Tracy graced the front page of the *Sunday News*, which always came wrapped in its comics section, for over 45 years, an all-time record.

Further proof of Patterson's genius is that of this nucleus of 10 strips around which the Chicago Tribune–Daily News Syndicate was built, five are still being syndicated. They are Gasoline Alley, Winnie Winkle, Moon Mullins, Annie (formerly Little Orphan Annie), and of course Dick Tracy.

You will notice that Waugh included in Dick Tracy's appeal a fascination with the criminal, the morbid and the bizarre. The *Sunday News* today still publishes a regular weekly feature, supported with photos, called "The Justice Story," a recap of sensational crime stories. What happens in Dick Tracy often pales by comparison.

Captain Patterson had a gut feeling that America was ready for Dick Tracy, a name he modified from Gould's initial "Plainclothes Tracy." The word "Dick" at the time was slang for a detective. In fact, the early dialogue in Dick Tracy was full of slang.

Dick Tracy was born in the dawn of the golden age of newspaper comic adventure strips. In the 1930's almost half the strips published were continuity strips. This trend continued through World War II before shifting to the advantage of humor strips, both sophisticated humor and what cartoonists call "big foot," such as the slapstick fun of Beetle Baily.

It is to the credit of Captain Patterson and the Chicago Tribune–Daily News Syndicate that they allowed their artists the widest range of personal drawing styles. Many syndicates wanted all their strips to have a certain look, but not Patterson.

This classic daily strip from October 14, 1949, presents not only a thoroughly reprehensible villainess but also psychological terror and Tracy's two-way wrist radio in action.

Following the undoing of "The Brain," Gould used some humor in the squad room to help the transition into a new story. The Brain's hat was the same shape and configuration as his head. However, Chief Patton seems less than thrilled with his new crown.

Visually, Dick Tracy was not interchangeable with Terry and the Pirates, or Smilin' Jack, On Stage, Gasoline Alley, or Brenda Starr. Even today this hallmark remains with Tribune Media Services. Compare its adventure strips with those of King Features. "The Phantom," "Mandrake the Magician," and "Flash Gordon" are all molded into a similar style.

The syndicate's policy of individual style was used by Chester Gould to the fullest. The artwork in Dick Tracy was never static; it was always changing. As the years went on, Gould's pen line thickened and he became increasingly interested in design and in simplifying drawings to their basic elements. It was a style that took years to form.

Adventure, crime, sexy women, perilous situations, violence, the same menu offered by the mass market tabloids of yesterday and today served Chester Gould well from the beginning. When he began Dick Tracy, Gould knew little of police procedure. However, he learned, and soon proper police procedure and scientific advances, both real and imagined, joined the mix.

A unique aspect of cartooning is that the complete cartoonist is both author and artist. Chester Gould developed into a master storyteller. So much so that mystery writer Ellery Queen tagged Dick Tracy as "fiction's first procedural detective." Gould never had any ghost writers helping him on Dick Tracy. He did have some assistants on artwork over the years, but that is a common practice in cartooning, where the deadline calls for top quality, exciting and interesting comics 365 days a year, year in and year out.

Cartoon historian and critic Maurice Horn has made some observations in his introduction to 75 Years of the Comics (Boston Book & Art, 1971) that are of interest in balancing the importance of Gould's writing versus his art:

"Narration, however defined, remains the essence of the comics; their purpose is to tell a story (or joke)....The literary qualities present in the comics...are not so readily apparent as are their graphic qualities....The comics are indeed a literary form, but one that should not be reduced to its literary elements, lest we subvert its very raison d'etre....The problem of creating a milieu at once ordinary and different is the lot of all mass media that aspire to become art forms."

Chester Gould's wide-ranging influence on the entire range of action-adventure comics and the image of the detective bear witness to his success as an innovator. His choice of wardrobe for Tracy, the trench coat and snapbrim fedora, became the trademark not just of Tracy but of most hardboiled tough-as-nails detectives, whether with the police or as private eyes.

Gould's influence is even seen in cartooning's radical avant-garde, underground cartoonists who flourished in the 1970s. Clay Geerdes, underground comics chronicler, notes that "Dick Tracy was the major influence on Spain Rodriquez's early work for *The East Village Other*. Strips such as "Trashman" and "Manning" show many Gouldian touches. Spain collects Dick Tracy."

"Talk to me, talk to me," plays the Brain as Chester Gould presents yet another way to make a woman sing for her life. His inventiveness and twists of his criminals' personalities always kept the reader wondering what would happen next.

The reality Gould pursued was escapist. He always considered his job to be part of the entertainment industry. While the surroundings, the police techniques, sometimes even the crimes were totally realistic, his characters, as is the custom in the comics, were larger than life. The good were good. The bad were evil.

The continual mystery and suspense in Gould's Dick Tracy kept the reader at a high level of excitement. But the excitement is tempered by the knowledge that right will triumph, that the extravagant or bizarre villain will be undone.

Dick Tracy's popularity in newspapers across the country mushroomed as Gould's detective entered into three areas that were not only highly lucrative to cartoonist and syndicate, but did wonders to spread the mythology of Dick Tracy and the recognition of America's most famous detective into every home.

The areas were merchandising, movies and the radio.

As early as May 1932 (Dick Tracy began publication in October 1931.), the New York *Daily News* in-house publication "News Pix" wrote: "A new *News* promotion idea, that of giving school children small buttons bearing a picture of the color comic character, Dick Tracy, and the word 'Detective,' has turned out to be a big success." Commercially licensed Dick Tracy items soon began to appear.

David Longest, author of the two-volume *Character Toys and Collectibles* (Collector Books, Box 3009, Paducah, KY 42001), notes that radio was the single most popular entertainment medium of the 1930's and 1940's. Remembering that Tracy was not only on the radio but also in the Saturday afternoon serial adventure cliff-hangers, one can see how a whole generation of American youth became Dick Tracy fans.

Sheet music was just one aspect of Chester Gould's attack on the mass media. Movies, radio, television and all types of merchanising helped support Tracy's tremendous popular appearl. The naturally strong graphics created by Chester Gould have made Dick Tracy collectible items some of the most attractive and sought after.

Within five years of Gould's creation of Dick Tracy, his hero was headed for Hollywood. The Tracy serial films of the 1930's were fast-paced, full of action, and very well received by their youthful audience.

Longest notes that on any Monday night in 1938, Dick Tracy at 5 P.M. on the NBC RED network lead off an evening of radio entertainment that offered in sequence: "Terry and the Pirates," "Jack Armstrong," and "Little Orphan Annie." Then at 6:30

P.M. the radio news and adult programming took over. "Amos 'n' Andy," "Uncle Ezra," and "Burns and Allen" followed the news.

The high design quality of Chester Gould's artwork and the immediately identifiable profile of Dick Tracy resulted in some strikingly bold and now highly collectable Tracy toys.

Comic character toy expert Longest lists as a favorite toy "The Dick Tracy Automatic

Modern merchandising of Dick Tracy includes some of the same products that have been associated with the strip since the beginning. Button-Up of Troy, Michigan, produces buttons, and the earliest promotion premium was a button issued in 1932. The rack toys by JA-RU of Jacksonville, Florida, include some nostalgic favorites, such as the I.D. set with clicker gun, the TV watch, and metal handcuffs with trick locking mechanism.

Police Station Complete with Squad Car," to quote the copy on the toy's outside box. The toy was manufactured by Marx Toy Co. and the outside box was 6″ × 9″ × 3″. Inside a bright lithographed tin police station with green plastic doors held the squad car. If you wound up the spring and pushed the release, the car, fully lithographed with Tracy characters, would shoot out.

Other toys included "Dick Tracy's Sparkling Riot Car with Siren," a lithographed tin 6½″ long friction-driven vehicle; "Dick Tracy Jr.'s Click Pistol;" the Dick Tracy Playing Card Game; pop-up book, coloring books, Big Little Books, comic books, submachine gun, miniature lead figures, detective kits, and a host of items not even cataloged.

However, the golden-haired Sparkle Plenty, the beautiful child born with a full head of hair to Gravel Gertie and B.O. Plenty, had to be the jackpot in merchandising for all of the Dick Tracy items. *Life* magazine even reported the phenomenon, as Sparkle Plenty instantly won the hearts of Dick Tracy's 26 million readers in 1947.

The joy with which America greeted the baby Sparkle Plenty was observed with interest by William M. McDuffee, manager of Gimbel's department store's toy department. McDuffee prevailed upon Ideal Toy Co. to manufacture a Baby Sparkle Plenty doll under license from the Chicago Tribune—Daily News Syndicate. Within 48 days, production of the dolls began.

The dolls went on sale July 28, 1947, at $5.98 apiece, and 10,000 were sold in the first five days. Ultimately about $3 million in Baby Sparkle Plenty dolls were purchased. This success lead to a Bonnie Braids doll when Tracy and Tess had a child, and later a Honeymoon doll, when Junior Tracy and Moon Maid had a baby. However, none of these could challenge the national fad associated with Baby Sparkle Plenty.

Dick Tracy toys are certainly not a thing of the past. Today, JA-RU, the rack toy company, from Jacksonville, Florida, has licensed a whole line of often wonderfully nostalgic inexpensive toys. Available are such favorites as a Dick Tracy Gun & I.D. Set, complete with clicker action on the gun; Dick Tracy Metal Handcuffs; Dick Tracy TV Watch; and Dick Tracy Crime Lab, among others.

International Concepts of New York City has been licensed to manufacture a full line of Dick Tracy and other comic character T-shirts and fun fashions. A midwest firm, Button Up Co., has focused on some of Gould's bizarre characters to fill up a 39-button display cardboard with 1¼″ full-color buttons. While there are old favorite images such as Tracy with his wrist TV, a more New Wave playfulness has Flattop saying on a button, "Shut up and dance," or Moon Maid saying, "Give it a rest."

Over the years there have been a number of working two-way wrist radios produced as toys. In the 1960's Remco manufactured a set of "Official Dick Tracy 2-Way Wrist Radios: 2 complete stations, strong signal buzzer, good up to ½ mile, battery powered." The box art showed Tracy and Junior communicating to each other with the bulky 5″ long two-way wrist radios. However, in recent years the most interesting Dick Tracy wrist merchandise was not a radio but a watch.

There had been many Tracy watches before it, but this one produced in the late 1970's was special. It was high-tech all the way. The packaging was a clear plastic Space Coupe, and contained along with the watch a mini-sized full-color illustrated instruction book. Dick Tracy's face graced the top of the watch but the most remarkable function of the watch was not showing the time. Rather it was the animated figure landing on the moon from the Space Coupe and waving the American flag while patriotic music played.

Chester Gould thought that watch was terrific. However, Tribune Media Licensing reports that the company making the watch is out of business and leftover inventory was most likely "dumped" in the Asian market.

With Dick Tracy using a two-way wrist TV-computer since summer 1986, the time is certainly right for some enterprising company to license a Dick Tracy wrist-computer.

Chester Gould's accomplishments rank him in that small group of cartoon superstars that have literally molded part of 20th-century popular culture. He certainly came a long way from his boyhood in Pawnee, Oklahoma. However, he never left his Oklahoma roots far behind him.

Riley Miller, his grandfather on his

International Concepts of New York City has been licensed by Tribune Media Services to manufacture not only T-shirts of Dick Tracy, Brenda Starr, Broomhilda and other TMS characters, but also a whole fashion line. These prototype designs are by Simon Lieberman, International Concept's designer.

mother's side, had made the trek out to Oklahoma to stake a claim and build a log cabin in 1892. His grandfather Gould was a minister who moved west from West Virginia.

Chester was born November 20, 1900, to Alice Miller Gould and Gilbert R. Gould. His mother lived to be part of a 1950's ritual for American celebrities, the honoring of her son on the October 22, 1958, broadcast of "This Is Your Life." During the half-hour show Gould met several persons he had not seen for nearly 50 years, including Mrs. Oliver A. Harker, who as Miss Bertha Kilpatrick was his first school teacher in Pawnee, Oklahoma, in 1906. Also on hand were four early schoolmates

he hadn't seen since 1919, including Walter Harrison, former publisher of the *Daily Oklahoman,* who was the first person to buy a cartoon from Gould.

As a youth Chester Gould was responsible for a small truck farm. And he enjoyed rural living. The urge to become a cartoonist struck him at age seven. It came partly as a result of the enjoyment he witnessed as townspeople viewed some of his sketches in the windows of his father's paper, the *Pawnee Courier Dispatch.*

His father encouraged him to draw from life, and suggested that young Chester go over to the Pawnee County courthouse and sketch some of the local Democratic party bigwigs who were in session. The drawings

This self-caricature of Chester Gould and Dick Tracy is copyrighted 1942 and was drawn for Martin Sheridan's book *Comics and Their Creators,* one of the earlier books to contain interviews with a wide variety of newspaper cartoonists. The original drawing of a similar self-caricature by Ernie "Nancy" Bushmiller for the same book sold for $450 at auction in New York City in the spring of 1986.

LISTEN, THERE'S GOT TO BE MORE ACTION. — BETTER STORY, SHORTER BALLOONS — AND BETTER LOOKING GIRL CHARACTERS.

Copyright 1942 by Chicago Tribune

were crude, but the persons drawn were recognizable. His dad pointed out who was who and taped the drawings in the front window of the print shop facing the town square.

Pawnee was a small town back then and had no postal carrier system. Everybody had to go to the Post Office to pick up their own mail. Chester's father's print shop was next to the Post Office. As the other side of the square had no businesses, just a livery stable, the town's citizens walked right in front of Chester's first art show.

The recognition he received made him decide that "This [cartooning] is for me."

As a youth Chester did odd art jobs around town; sign painting and spot art for the local paper always kept a little change in his pocket. He also worked as a soda jerk at Jay's Drug Store where he earned $15 a week when he could work from 7 A.M. to 7 P.M.

His first cartoon to receive national attention came in 1916 when he won a contest by *The American Boy* magazine for a patriotic cartoon. World War I was the topic.

Chester won the contest, $10, and the right to have his cartoon published in the magazine, for his treatment of a boy in a cornfield watching a troop of soldiers marching down a dirt road. The boy is hoeing corn, which was a hot, hot job. One soldier's eyes meet with the boy's eyes, and the caption read, "What a Stint He's Got." Each coveted the other's job.

During his boyhood Chester was reading Mutt and Jeff, The Katzenjammer Kids, Mama's Angel Child, Hairbreath Harry, Little Nemo, Slim Jim, Buster Brown and any other newspaper comic he could find. His dad would buy the *Daily Oklahoman* from Oklahoma City, and that was his daily comics source.

Of all the strips he read, including those that appeared in the Chicago *Tribune,* which his father sometimes bought as a special treat, Mutt and Jeff was his favorite. Chester decided he wanted to be a "big-time cartoonist." So at age seven, while idolizing the Bud Fisher art in Mutt and Jeff and having his own small success as an artist in Pawnee, Chester had set his course to be a cartoonist.

After high school Chester attended Oklahoma A&M in Stillwater for two years. It's now known as Oklahoma State. There he studied commerce and marketing. He joined Pi Alpha fraternity, and as always he drew cartoons and took any type of art jobs he could rustle up. He illustrated a fraternity pledge book and drew for the yearbook.

While at Oklahoma A&M, Gould began having editorial cartoons published by the *Tulsa Democrat.* He also drew sports cartoons for the *Daily Oklahoman* every other week.

But Chicago was calling him. Chester became restless in Oklahoma. The Chicago Tribune Syndicate headed by Captain Joseph Patterson was the hottest thing in the new burgeoning syndicated cartoon field. Chester wanted to be where the action was.

He arrived in Chicago on September 1, 1921, with $50 cash in his pocket and a suitcase full of samples of his published work in Oklahoma newspapers. Gould would turn 21 on November 20, 1921. The ten-year struggle to become a top syndicated cartoonist had begun.

Shortly after he arrived, his mother began reading about gangsters and shootouts in Chicago. She wrote Chester a letter, which included, among other things, the plea, "I've just read in the newspaper about those gangsters in Chicago who have been shooting and robbing people for no reason at all, and you with $50 in your pocket. Come home at once."

Chester Gould, his mind set on becoming a famous cartoonist, ignored his mother's wishes. By the time her letter arrived, he had already found himself a job, albeit a temporary one, on the Chicago *Journal.*

There were five daily newspapers in Chicago in 1921 and at first all five had turned Gould down. His portfolio of art and tear sheets from Oklahoma was nice but lacked the maturity needed for "Big City" cartooning, the editors told him.

Gould's chance at the Chicago *Journal,* an evening paper, came when a fellow in the art department had an appendectomy. Chester was just in the right place at the right time. So after less than a week in Chicago, Chester Gould was making $30 a week, and working for a major daily paper. The job only lasted a month, but it certainly must have lifted his spirits and was an excellent credit.

But jobs at newspapers just dried up for

A Chester Gould sports cartoon about Gil Berry, the University of Illinois football star, dates from his early days in Chicago.

the unemployed Gould. He tried the *Tribune,* his preferred choice, and the *Herald Examiner,* the *Post,* and the *Evening American* without success. He even inquired about a job at an A&P grocery store on Vaughn Avenue as a stock boy, but fortunately for all of us that job was filled.

However, good luck followed Gould throughout his career, and a fellow named Haggerty, whom he'd met several times in a cigar store, tipped him off about an opening in a small art studio on South Dearborn Street.

After being hired at the Zuckerman Studio in the fall of 1921, Gould would spend almost a year there. The work wasn't all that stimulating, consisting mostly of mundane stock advertising for things such as "Spring Sale." As Gould was a cartoonist and not a trained commercial illustrator, he became a glorified office boy. His duties included carting artwork to the engravers, pasting down artwork, erasing and the like. He still kept making the rounds of the newspapers and larger art studios.

Gould supported himself on a $15 a week salary from the Zuckerman Studio, and was soon drawing for the studio. One job he remembers in particular was drawing a coffee cake every afternoon for a client who owned a bakery. The fresh cake would arrive at 3 P.M. and the drawing had to be at the engraver's at 4 P.M. to make the deadline for the next paper. Then the staff ate the cake.

His next good fortune came when the *Tribune's* Copy and Art Service Department hired him for $50 a week, a fortune compared to his former salary. The Copy and Art Service did spot art for small advertisers. It wasn't what Gould wanted but it was at the *Tribune* and he was making a good salary.

Nothing ever seemed to discourage Chester Gould in his quest to become a syndicated cartoonist. But he had more than hard working going for him. He was at times bold and inventive in pursuing his goal.

As he seemed locked into the advertising side of the *Tribune*, Gould set his sights on the Hearst newspaper, the *American*.

The editor of the *American*, a man named Curley, kept putting him off about his cartoon work, or he'd refer Gould to King Features Syndicate, owned by Hearst, in New York City. He was pleasant enough, but got Gould nowhere.

It happened that the *American*, edited by Curley, published a cartoon on the back of the paper that Gould despised. He didn't think it was funny or even well drawn. The strip was called "Joys and Glooms," and was the work of T.E. Powers.

Gould decided he could improve on the cartoon and boldly put a plan into action. He sketched his own cartoon and then, although not employed by the *American*, took it to that newspaper's own engraving department, bluffed them and had the cartoon made into a plate. Then he had a proof pulled and pasted his cartoon on top of Powers' in the day's newspaper.

By observation, Gould knew when Curley would be out of the office and when Curley's secretary, a formidable Miss Dougherty, would also be absent. While the scrub woman was cleaning, Gould, in shirtsleeves so he looked like an employee of the *American*, nonchalantly strolled into Curley's office and placed the paper with the bogus Powers cartoon on his desk.

Later that day Gould was asked to come to Curley's office. The editor admitted he'd almost been fooled. He said that the only way to get rid of Gould was to hire him, which he did on the spot for $10 more a week than Gould was making in the *Tribune's* Copy and Art Service Department.

Gould worked at the *American* from 1923 into part of 1929. He and Curley developed a good working relationship. One issue of the *American* even had 11 different cartoons and spot drawings by Gould.

The *American's* publisher William Randolph Hearst was trying to hire for King Features the cartoonist Ed Wheelan, whose strip, "Minute Movies," was very popular. However, Wheelan was happy where he was. This resulted in Curley requesting that Gould develop the comic strip "Fillum Funnies." The hero was Jack Storm, the female lead Dolly Darling and the villain George O. Silverrough.

It rankled Gould's creative spirit to produce a comic strip that was really an imitation of another more popular one, but he complied. "Fillum Funnies" was published in the Chicago *American* and later also in Hearst's New York *Journal*. However, King Features turned it down for syndication.

The other strip Gould created for the Chicago *American* was "Radio Cats." At the time the most common radios were crystal sets. These radios had a part, nicknamed "cat's whiskers" by the public, which had to be adjusted to receive broadcasts. That was the inspiration for the name. "Radio Cats" was a humor strip featuring Siamese cats.

Gould has said that upon arriving in

Immediately prior to beginning Dick Tracy, Gould drew "The Girl Friends," for the Chicago *Daily News*. The strip from August 14, 1931, about two months before Tracy debuted, is typical. Note that the blonde is very similar to Tess Trueheart and the gentleman caller has Tracy's profile.

Chicago, the work he found to support himself was only his first job. His second job, and a goal he considered paramount, was to complete his college education. He had completed only two years at Oklahoma A&M.

Although Chester Gould had a burning desire to be a successful cartoonist, he was always a businessman. He enrolled at Northwestern University in Evanston, Illinois, the town immediately north of Chicago. His degree would be earned in Commerce and Marketing.

The elevated train provided easy mass transportation and Gould found lodgings in Wilmette, the town north of Evanston. He'd commute to downtown Chicago and work at the *American*, and then go to school at night.

It was not uncommon for families with a vacant room to rent to students, and Gould boarded with the Thrumston family, whom he enjoyed. June Thrumston, the daughter, thought Gould was lonely and convinced him to go on a blind date with her best friend, Edna Gauger. For 25-year-old Chester Gould it was love at first sight. He even phoned and woke Edna up at 8:30 A.M. the morning after that first date to say what a wonderful time he'd had.

Unlike Dick Tracy, who took 18 years to marry Tess Trueheart, Chester Gould proposed within three months. The marriage was in 1926. In the short autobiography that Gould would include in his National Cartoonists Society directory, he listed his marriage to Edna as an achievement equal to creating Dick Tracy. The couple had a daughter Jean, and in turn two grandchildren, Tracy Richard O'Connell and Susie O'Connell.

By 1928, Gould was making $100 a week. That was considered excellent money at the time. However, his career goal of becoming a "big time" cartoonist seemed stalled. He had regional success in Chicago, but wanted national syndication from coast to coast.

Jean Gould O'Connell says her dad would say, "Failure isn't in my vocabulary." He kept submitting new comic strips ideas to the various syndicates and they kept rejecting them.

For the *American* he created a new strip, "Why It's a Windy City," in which he sketched and interviewed "big shots, businessmen and celebrities." These included Eddie Cantor, Al Jolson and Ed Wynn.

As a young man Gould had endless energy. He claimed, "The Lord gave me one hell of a good body." At the *American* the four other staff artists would depart after the newspaper, an afternoon paper, came off the press. However, Gould would sit at his drawing board and continue to work on new ideas for possible syndication. During this time Hearst was looking for a new artist for "Little Annie Rooney," King Features' entry in competition with "Little Orphan Annie." However, Gould wanted only to create his own original concept.

After leaving the *American*, Gould worked for the Chicago *Daily News* at a cut in pay where he created "The Girl Friends," what in the trade is called "a pretty girl strip." It was his major regional comic strip between "Fillum Fables" and Dick Tracy.

Gould always gravitated toward the Chicago *Tribune*. Possibly it was because he had been so impressed by the *Tribune's* comics as a boy having only an occasional opportunity to read the paper. At this point, with reasonable regional success, he made an appointment to see Captain Joseph Patterson, to see if a face-to-face meeting might be the key to impressing the Captain that his work was worth national syndication.

Captain Patterson, who by late 1930 was spending most of his time in New York City, was cordial to Gould. None of Gould's current work was appropriate to his needs at the moment, but he encouraged Gould to send him more work. He also mentioned as an afterthought that he was seeking a new editorial cartoonist for the New York *Daily News*.

That was all the encouragement Gould needed. He again put into action an innovative plan to secure for himself the editorial cartoonist's job in New York. Gould spent what he recalls to be about $50 to have the *Sunday* and *Daily News* sent to him in Chicago by first class mail. He focused on the editorial page to analyze Patterson's journalistic point of view. Then he would draw an editorial cartoon as he would have drawn if he'd been on the *News's* staff.

For thirty consecutive days, including weekends, Gould personally delivered his editorial cartoon, neatly packaged and addressed to Captain Patterson, New York *Daily News*, 220 East 42nd St., New York,

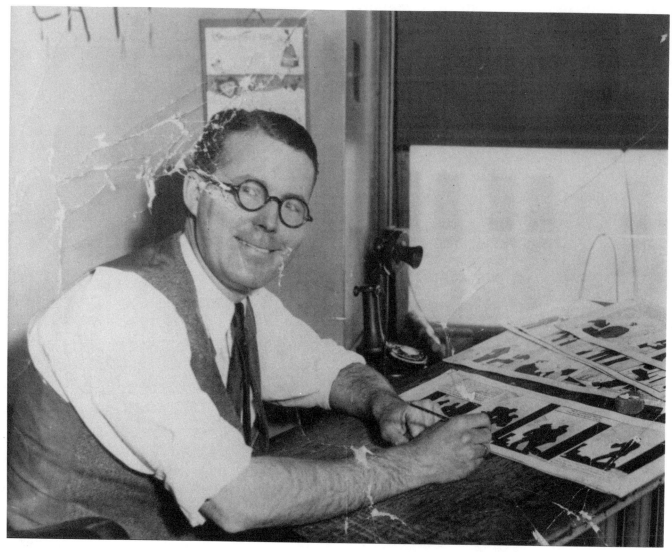

Dick Tracy had been syndicated on October 4, 1931, and Chester Gould, age 31, is shown with the daily strip for March 28, 1932, on his drawing board and wearing a big smile. He'd become syndicated after ten years of trying. (Photo courtesy of the Gould family.)

NY, to the mail car of the famed railroad train the Twentieth Century Limited. This assured overnight delivery from Chicago to New York.

Gould had no patience for artists who wanted to live in a garret and suffer for their art. He thought they were "jerks." Instead, when on business in Chicago, Gould dressed for success. He claimed that he tried to dress like a banker. The effect worked, for after a few days the staff of the Twentieth Century Limited mail car thought Gould was a big shot sending important stuff to Captain Patterson.

In the end the editorial cartooning job at the New York *Daily News* went to C.D. Batchelor, an artist with what Gould called "a breezy, sketchy" style. However, Gould

received a personal note from Captain Patterson:

"I thank you so much for letting me see the cartoons which came every day. They are not quite what I'm looking for but please see that I get any other material that you might think I would be interested in."

As far as Gould was concerned such encouragement equalled hitting paydirt. He told his wife Edna that he would soon have a job with Captain Patterson. In the winter of 1931, Gould began to dream up Plainclothes Tracy.

Chicago and gangsters had become synonymous in the Prohibition era, and Gould thought about the possibilities of a modern Sherlock Holmes set in this period. Gould figured the public, like himself, was fed up with crooked judges, crooked lawyers, hoodlums, and gangsterism.

Plainclothes Tracy featured tough talk, slang, and a bad guy who was seriously evil, the villain named Cleaver, who reappeared as Big Boy in the Dick Tracy strip. In the first episode Cleaver is torturing information from a hood by applying a torch to his bare feet. Acting on a tip, Tracy and other detectives burst in. Cleaver had escaped moments before and the cliffhanger has Tracy hot on his trail.

It is interesting that Tracy wears a straw boater hat in the trial strips, but by the first published strip on Sunday, October 4, 1931, he is wearing his now famous snap-brim fedora.

Weeks and months went by and Gould heard nothing from Captain Patterson. Then a telegram arrived August 18, 1931. "BELIEVE PLAINCLOTHES TRACY HAS POSSIBILITIES...SEE ME IN CHICAGO THE TWENTIETH...CALL MY SECRETARY FOR TIME."

When Edna Gould called her husband at

'Plainclothes Tracy," the Trial Strip That Became Dick Tracy

work and read the telegram to him, Chester was drawing an oriental rug for an ad in the Chicago *Daily News.* After hearing the telegram he couldn't draw, because his hand was shaking so much. He asked a fellow artist named Hatton to finish the drawing.

Two days later, Gould, dressed in a new suit, appeared for his appointment with Captain Patterson in the Tribune Tower building. Patterson was in shirtsleeves, without a necktie, and Gould distinctly remembered he was wearing old Army shoes.

The Captain changed "Plainclothes" to "Dick" Tracy and asked Gould if he could have two weeks completed by September 1, 1931. After 10 years of trying, Chester Gould's chance had come.

Paterson gave Gould the raw plot outline for the first story. According to Gould, the Captain said that Tracy should be dating this girl whose father owned a delicatessen and lived with his family upstairs over the store. The old man, who put his receipts in a cigar box under his bed, is robbed and killed. Gould would take it from there.

Gould never gave any thought to or ever hinted at what Tracy was prior to joining the police force, other than that he was a nice young fellow about 25-years-old. "Dick," as selected by Patterson, was slang for a detective. "Tracy," as chosen by Gould as the hero's name, was a play on the word "tracing," for tracking down criminals.

For two weeks Chester Gould drew constantly, taking time off only to catnap. The saga of Dick Tracy had begun, and Gould alone would write it until Max Allan Collins took over the writing chores upon Gould's retirement in late December 1977. Initially the Sunday and daily strips did not follow the same story.

The first Dick Tracy published was in the Detroit *Mirror* on Sunday, October 4, 1931. The second appeared a week later, also in the Detroit *Mirror.* On Monday, October 12, 1931, the daily strip began in the New York *Daily News.* The Sunday pages did not merge with the daily continuity until May 29, 1932.

To learn more about criminology, Gould studied at the crime detection laboratory in Chicago, which was then part of Northwestern University, his alma mater. (In 1931 the police didn't have their own crime

The First Appearance of Dick Tracy

lab.) He also hired Al Valandis, a retired policeman and one of the first police artists in the country, to help him depict police procedure properly.

Even the first published Dick Tracy had carefully designed black areas that were to become trademarks of the strip. It also had a clever Tracy who deduces from how a "woman" ducks a punch he's thrown that she isn't a woman at all, but "Pinkie the Stabber, ex-boxer and stick-up ace." Pinkie tries to punch out Tracy and gets a two-fisted hello.

Standing over the flattened hoodlum, Tracy says, "Well, there's your man, Chief—and when it comes to women, all I can say is you pick 'em rough—plenty rough."

Chester Gould always believed in the visual power of the newspaper. The tools available were the photograph and the cartoon. He set himself the task of out-doing every cartoonist in the business. He stated his theory was to "stifle all competition."

At first many of Gould's stories were inspired by news items about Al Capone, Dillinger, Bonnie and Clyde, Baby Face Nelson and other criminals. He also did a version, but with a happy ending, of the Lindbergh kidnapping. It was Gould's desire to beat the competition that brought the bizarre villain into being. Not only did the villains fascinate his readers, they resulted in Dick Tracy being talked about in news columns. Over the years much of the publicity about Dick Tracy was initiated not by the syndicate but by Gould himself.

In 1935 Gould bought 130 acres in rural Woodstock, Illinois, about 65 miles north-west of Chicago. A year later he and Edna had the old farmhouse on the land incorporated into a new house they built. Thirty years later, at age 66, Gould completely remodeled the house. How many men do you know who would redo their home at age 66?

It was no accident that Gould bought a farm. During the Great Depression, many economic advisers suggested the best way to insulate yourself from the ravages of another Depression was to own a farm. Chester Gould's boyhood had included work on a five-acre farm in Oklahoma, and he took the advice to heart. Also his good friend Al Lowenthal, who had been his agent in his freelance days, had purchased two farms, one near Waukegan and the other near Merringo. Lowenthal suggested Woodstock as a possible location.

Lowenthal was also instrumental in the introduction of Sam Catchem as Dick Tracy's sidekick and fellow detective. The first story with Sam Catchem is reprinted in this volume.

"You ought to have a Jewish detective in there," said Lowenthal one day to Gould. Lowenthal himself was Jewish and who knows if he was being serious or not. Well, Gould took him seriously and Sam Catchem, who first appeared in December 1948, was the result.

As far as Gould was concerned, Woodstock and his home in the Bull Valley section was heaven on earth. He even drew a special portrait of Dick Tracy which the local chamber of commerce used on its letterhead. Tracy says, "I live here and like

The counterfeit cigarette stamp ring loses a member when they try to rub out a key witness in the case against them. Gould never pussyfooted about violence, but never used it gratuitously either. If it fit the story, he didn't shy away from it.

"I LIVE HERE AND LIKE IT!"

it." Woodstock, which is a lovely town, has a central square patterned after the square in Woodstock, Vermont.

When he and Edna first drove over deeply rutted dirt roads to view their property in 1935, all that stood on it was a ramshackle tumbledown farmhouse and barn. Gould, who had been born in a one-room cabin with a dirt floor in Oklahoma, wasn't bothered.

"Chet succeeded in everything he did," stated Edna Gould. "Nothing daunted him."

When the house was remodeled in 1966, the style chosen was contemporary country casual, featuring Indiana bluestone and cedar wood. Jean Gould O'Connell remembers her parents were as excited about the building as a couple of newlyweds.

"They'd go out with their coffee in the morning and sit on the piles of lumber and hold hands," she remembers.

Remodeled, the house featured four bedrooms, five bathrooms, including what Gould called "The Grotto," a curving rock-lined hallway with a small waterfall that led to the regal guest bathroom, and an enclosed, heated Olympic-size swimming pool. The house, set on 60 of the 130 acres owned by Gould, is surrounded by a five-hole golf course. There are six fireplaces and three working wells, plus a windmill and a gas-powered electrical generator in its own small building in case of emergencies. Upstairs the most striking feature is the rotunda bar whose floor rotates a full 360 degrees every 45 minutes.

After Gould's death in May 1985 at the age of 84, the family believed there were just too many memories attached to the house, so they decided to sell the property, which was listed with a realtor for $1.2 million. The remaining 70 acres of farmland were also available for an additional $300,000.

Chester Gould left Oklahoma in 1921 convinced he would succeed, and indeed he did become "a big time cartoonist," in fact one of the most popular of his day.

Once Dick Tracy became a runaway success, Gould, like many cartoonists, found that producing a comic strip 365 days a year was a demanding task. His first assistant was Dick Moores who would later take over the "Gasoline Alley" comic strip and with his own personal style make it one of the best-drawn strips in syndications. Later assistants would include Russell Stamm, Carl Anderson, Jack Ryan, his brother Ray Gould, Dick Locher, and finally

The ability to constantly vary the basic theme of Dick Tracy with new gimmicks, in this case Claude Crystal on ice, is how Gould was able to hook his readership year after year.

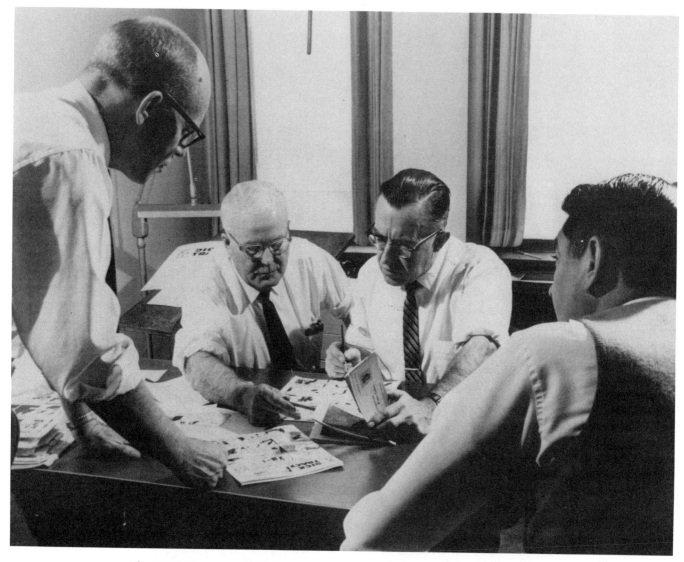

The Dick Tracy creative team in 1963 included (left to right) Gould's brother Ray, his letterer; Chester Gould; Jack Ryan; and Rick Fletcher.

Rick Fletcher. They would help on ruling, lettering, and backgrounds and whatever else Gould required. Gould always conducted the production of Dick Tracy as a business. Sure it was fun and he loved it, but the pressures of deadline were always there and the strip was drawn in an orderly fashion on a schedule set by Gould. Nothing was arbitrarily assigned an artist. Gould was involved personally in the production until his retirement.

There are numerous theories on reasons for the phenomenal success of Dick Tracy. But one point all critics agree on is that it crackled with an incredible tension. Gould kept his readers guessing as to what would happen. Some even contend that Dick Tracy, instead of being the star of the strip, really took a secondary role to the villains, those crazed grotesque rogues who caused

an astonishing variety of crime and displayed amazing malevolence. With Gould's acknowledged purpose of letting Dick Tracy "fight it out face to face with crooks via the hot lead route," the inexorable doom of the hoodlum was assured. Still the death of contract killer Flattop brought floral arrangements and sympathy cards to the syndicate's offices.

If much of the American heritage is built upon the Puritan work ethic, Dick Tracy is a proper hero, incorruptible, hard working, and able to stir himself into a righteous fury in his fight against crime. His popular screen and radio show image, combined with his daily appearance in newspapers, captured the imagination of a whole generation of boys. These kids could identify with Junior Tracy. He was their age. They could join him and his youthful

Crimestoppers in their imaginations.

The near triumph of evil in Dick Tracy has more appeal for adults, however. All adults know that Dick Tracy will triumph; what they don't know is how. This is the key to the classic Dick Tracy story: the crime, the chase, the capture.

Chester Gould considered Captain Patterson a teacher, a person who had an incredible talent for finding the pulse of the American public. At times in Dick Tracy's history Gould hit the jackpot himself, as with the marriage of Gravel Gertie and B.O. Plenty and their offspring Sparkle Plenty. He also felt that Dick Tracy was not just crime and gloom, that any comic strip needed humor and human interest and family values, all of which he made plentiful in Tracy.

The Chicago *Tribune* was literally Gould's professional home and he felt tremendous loyalty to it. The *Tribune* gave him a lifetime contract and stock in the corporation. In the late 1940's Gould designed a special promotional who-done-it for the *Tribune*, "The Black Bag Mystery." Colonel McCornick, Patterson's cousin and head honcho at the *Tribune*, promised $1

Junior Tracy had been a very popular character in the strip since his creation as an Oliver Twist-type urchin whom Tracy adopts. In 1947, Gould invented "The Crimestoppers," a "sort of detective club," according to Junior. Soon Crimestoppers clubs were forming all over America, supported of course by Dick Tracy and Junior merchandising items.

903477

You're always right with AUTOLITE (Ford)

Gould did a series of four mini-mysteries for Ford Autolite batteries. The plots may have been a bit corny, but they were good fun. The wrist TV figures prominently in the storyline.

per new subscriber. "The Black Bag Mystery" brought in 50,000 new subscribers, but Gould refused the prize money.

"My reward has been in being in the Chicago *Tribune* and they have paid me over and over but I am proud and happy to do something to help my own paper," said Gould.

But McCormick wouldn't be thwarted completely. Gould was asked over to the *Tribune* garage on the pretense of seeing some new equipment. The whole board of directors of the *Tribune* were there. A large paper "box" was hidden in the shadows of the garage. When Gould arrived, he heard the throaty roar of an engine and Colonel McCormick himself drove a brand new Cadillac through the paper box and gave the car to Gould as a gesture of appreciation.

Later when Marshall Field of the rival Chicago *Sun-Times* decided to raid the Tribune Syndicate's group of top cartoonists, he found that Gould would not even listen to him. Gould has stated he didn't fear he could not have another success the size of Dick Tracy, but that his loyalty to the *Tribune* would in his own mind have made him feel like a traitor. A different opinion was held by Milton Caniff, who like Gould didn't own the character he drew for the *Tribune*.

In the winter of 1987 newsletter of the National Cartoonists Society, Caniff says, "From the very start it ["Terry and the Pirates"] belonged to the syndicate. There was no question of ownership. That's why I started 'Steve Canyon.' I was hoping somebody would come along and give me a chance to do just that. Marshall Field did in 1944. I had two years to go on my Terry and the Pirates contract, but I was glad to get a chance at a guarantee of ownership and editorial control. Field was willing to go for that. People were astounded that I would give up something like Terry, but I

didn't give up anything, because I didn't have anything. . . . I didn't own it."

Had Gould not felt so at home with the *Tribune* and so loyal to it, he might have jumped syndicates as Caniff did so successfully. Caniff was replaced by George Wunder, who wrote and drew "Terry and the Pirates" from 1947 until February 1973.

In honor of the 50th Anniversary of Dick Tracy (1981) the prestigious Graham Gallery on Madison Avenue, New York City, exhibited Chester Gould's first one-man show in an art gallery. He had in the fall of 1978 been the subject of a major retrospective at the Museum of Cartoon Art, Comly Ave., Rye Brook, New York, where he is a member of the Museum's Cartoon Hall of Fame. Any group show of important works of cartoon art by necessity must include works by Gould.

Ironically, the image of Dick Tracy first took the New York art world by storm in the early 1960's when Pop Art was in its infancy and Andy Warhol used Tracy and Sam Catchem as subjects for a major painting.

Pop Art is characteristically realistic in imagery; it is rooted in an urban environment (the founding fathers of Pop were residents of New York and London); and it considers comic strips and other things as "merely motifs" or excuses to do a painting.

Dick Tracy by Chester Gould is characteristically realistic and is also rooted in an urban setting. As to the argument about its being "merely motif," baloney is baloney any way you slice it.

Gould felt that the Pop Artists had hit upon a good gimmick and that Warhol's several Dick Tracy paintings and the notoriety they brought were good for the comic strip.

A further irony of Warhol's paintings of Dick Tracy and the hullabaloo about elevat-

This is a single Gould panel from Dick Tracy. Some people might think it a Pop Art painting by Lichtenstein. The connection between Chester Gould's artwork and Pop Art has assured him a place in art history far beyond that of most cartoonists.

ing cartoon images into fine art by isolating them as images, blowing them up to heighten design, making them painterly and hanging them in art galleries, is that Chester Gould's artwork didn't need any elevation. His art had already arrived years before.

Trendsetting cartoonists such as Chester Gould, who have earned more fame and fortune than most artists, almost seem to relish not being totally accepted by the fine art establishment. Part of the fun of being a cartoonist is having one foot in the establishment and the other on the wrong side of the tracks in terms of the artistic elite. Some critics consider cartooning the pimple on the fanny of illustration. But there are a lot of ignorant art critics.

In September 1983 *The New York Times* stated, "The cartoon, it would seem, has found recognition as a legitimate art form—that is to say, an indigenous 20th-century American folk art."

Georgia Reilly, for many years director of comic art at the Graham Gallery, has said that only since 1972, a decade after Warhol painted Dick Tracy, have cartoons appealed to serious collectors rather than social historians.

Chuck Green, executive director of the Museum of Cartoon Art, notes that European galleries and museums were showing American cartoon art years ahead of those in America. "The Europeans were also ahead of us in recognizing American jazz and film," says Green. "It's typical of a popular art form, a natural evolution, that the elite of a country overlook what the masses are doing."

The stark flat black areas, total absence of Benday dot patterns, solid forms bordered by a hard-edged line that developed from thin to thick over the years, all contributed to Gould's success in transmitting the moods he wanted in his art.

In later years Gould's cartoon panels would sometimes take commonplace im-

Panel text:
RLD NEEDS THIS FELLOW, LORD.

HIS SIMPLE FAITH AND HOMELY, DIRECT WAY STAND OUT LIKE A BEACON IN THESE CONFUSED DAYS.

WON'T YOU SAVE HIM? YOU'RE OUR ONLY HOPE. AMEN.

Reg. U. S. Pat. Off.; Copyright, 1950, by The Chicago Tribune

SOME PEOPLE HAVE SAID THEY DON'T LIKE B. O. PLENTY. WELL— WE DO! BUT ON THE OTHER HAND, WOULD GERTIE AND SPARKLE BE BETTER OFF WITH B. O. GONE?

WHAT DO YOU THINK?

Religious sentiment of a sincere, downhome nature has been a constant in Chester Gould's work from the beginning of Dick Tracy. When all else fails, or the moment calls for it, the cast of DickTracy get down on their knees and pray to God.

ages and present them as the focal points of the viewers' attention.

The only two projects Gould was personally involved in that might fit the classic definition of fine art were two limited edition prints. One was a color lithograph published by Abrams Original Editions in an edition of 100 prints and 10 artist's proofs signed and numbered by the artist. Released in 1978, the Gould piece along with that of Hal "Prince Valiant" Foster quickly sold out.

The second project was published in conjunction with the 500-copy edition of *The Fiftieth Anniversary Dick Tracy Scrapbook*. Gould himself signed the title page of the limited edition, 11″ × 17″ book which itself is an *objet d'art*. For the first 50 copies a 22″ × 29″ print, the same size as the Abrams print, was published, with 10 black-and-white proofs. The image, hand pulled from an old-fashioned line cut, was hand-watercolored, numbered and stamped with Gould's signature.

Gould's originals from Dick Tracy have until recently been collected by only a small circle of comic art collectors. However, since the shows at the Museum of Cartoon Art and the Graham Gallery, interest in Gould by collectors of Pop Art has increased, as has that of collectors of 20th-century American drawings. It is reasonable to project that within a decade most of the original Gould art available will have been absorbed into private and museum collections and the value of his originals will continue to increase significantly.

The significance of Chester Gould's ac-

complishments in the art world were highlighted by *New York Times* art critic John Russell at the time of the Graham Gallery show. He wrote:

"Looking at the originals of the Dick Tracy cartoons, we realize that this was the 'Dallas' of its day—the long running serial with which people loved to identify. Dick Tracy added excitement and continuity and a weird coherence to the lives of hundreds of thousands of people.

"And Chester Gould gave value for money. Rare is the novelist who could not learn something from the concision, the pace and the unfailing momentum of his dialogue. As for the image, we soon see that the emphasis—which was heavy—fell just where its weight was needed. He was a workman of a very high order in a craft that is much harder than it looks. The images survive surprisingly well as exhibition material, and as tokens of a time when issues were clear-cut, when law was law, order was order, and the best man won out in the end."

If it hadn't been for Dick Tracy, there's a good chance Li'l Abner Yokum would never have married Daisy Mae Scragg.

Dick Tracy was the inspiration for Al Capp's parody of America's most famous detective in his comic strip "Li'l Abner." "Fearless Fosdick" was Li'l Abner's "ideel," and appeared as a comic strip within a comic strip.

At the time Capp approached Chester Gould and asked permission to parody Tracy, he had done any number of one-shot

Gould took the last daily sequence from his trial strip "Plainclothes Tracy" and developed it into a sequence that was published in Dick Tracy on December 1 through December 4, 1931. The Big Boy character is patterned after Al Capone, and Texie Garcia, the speakeasy songstress, after Texas Guinan.

parodies. Most likely that's what Capp originally had planned. But sometimes a cartoon character assumes a life of its own. A recent case in point is the Lucky Eddie character in "Hagar the Horrible" by Dik Browne. Lucky Eddie was developed as just a funny character for a specific gag. However the chinless dunce's popularity has made him a regular in the Hagar cast of comic characters.

So it probably was with Fearless Fosdick. He just captured the imagination of Li'l Abner readers, the mail poured into Al Capp, and Fosdick became a fixture in Li'l Abner. In fact Capp used "Fearless Fosdick by Lester Gooch" so much that he could have sent Gould royalty checks.

At first Chester was happy for the free publicity, but as Fearless Fosdick kept returning to Li'l Abner year after year, he privately tired of the parody. Also the dubious honor of having his own name changed by Capp from Chester Gould to "Lester Gooch" most likely wore thin after awhile.

Still, Fearless Fosdick is as ingrained into American 20th-century popular culture as Dick Tracy. Both Al Capp and Chester Gould were cartoon geniuses. They had one-of-a-kind inventive minds. While Gould had his roster of villains, Al Capp gave the world Kickapoo Joy Juice, brewed by the hairy Hairless Joe and his native American sidekick, Lonesome Polecat; Sadie Hawkins Day, where women could catch men and then marry them; Lower Slobbovia, Capp's version of Russian Siberia; Senator Jack S. Phogbound, the Shmoos, the Kigmies, Evil Eye Fleegle and a host of beautiful women from Dogpatch. These included Moonbeam McSwine, simply gorgeous and odoriferous, as her daddy raised her with his hogs; the totally irresistible Stupifying Jones; and sometimes deadly Wolfgal; and the love of General Bullmoose's life, Appassionata von Climax—the name says it all.

So Dick Tracy's Capp-altered ego, Fearless Fosdick, brought about Li'l Abner's marriage after 18 years of lovely bachelorhood. Here's how.

Daisy Mae, ever looking for a ploy to capture the elusive Abner, brings the comics section of the newspaper to the young Yokum's attention.

"Look—in today's paper Fearless Fosdick proposed an' Prudence Pimpleton ac-

cepted," says Daisy Mae. Abner scoffs this off as a "usual comical strip trick, t'keep stupid readers excited."

However, Abner is reminded he has pledged to do whatever Fosdick does. So Abner drops to both knees and laughingly says, "Daisy Mae. Will yo'—ha-ha—marry me?"

With tears in her eyes, Daisy Mae responds, "Ah—SOB—will. (Oh, how mizzuble all this is. Th' biggest moment in mah life—an' it's jest a—SOB—joke fum a comical strip.") Well Daisy Mae gets the last laugh.

Fosdick is shown married in the strip within a strip and Abner doesn't even have time to get out of bed before he's surrounded by the bride, Mammy and Pappy Yokum and Marryin' Sam.

Abner is in disbelief. "This caint be happenin'—n-not after all th' y'ars ah has successfully d-dodged it."

Marryin' Sam will not be swayed from the task at hand. "An', so ah now pronounces yo': yo' panic stricken lout—an yo': yo' bootiful tremblin' young morsel, MAN AN' WIFE.—$1.35, please," says Sam.

While on his honeymoon, Li'l Abner discovers the Fosdick marriage was only a cruel dream sequence. Fosdick wakes up overjoyed. "Egad. There is no Mrs. Fosdick. I didn't marry my—ugh—loyal fiancée Prudence Pimpleton. There never was a rule that unmarried detectives would be fired. It was all a DREAM. I'M FREE—FREE."

Using his Dogpatch native wit, Li'l Abner yells, "Then—SO IS AH."

But he ain't.

He leaves Daisy Mae stranded in their flea-bag New York City honeymoon hotel and hightails it back to Dogpatch. Where the matriarch of the Yokum clan, Mammy, explains the facts of life to him.

"But, son—try to unnerstan'," she says. "Your marriage warn't no dream. It don't matter no more—whut Fosdick done done, or what Fosdick didn't done done. YO' IS MARRIED—HOPELESSLY—PERMANENTLY—MARRIED."

The Fosdick romance with Prudence Pimpleton lasted until the end of Li'l Abner in the late 1970's when Al Capp ended the strip shortly before his death. It was an engagement that outlasted both Dick Tracy's to Tess Trueheart and Li'l Abner's to Daisy Mae.

Dick Tracy has been on the receiving end

of many a bullet in his tenure under Chester Gould, and Al Capp parodied this by having Li'l Abner's "ideel" literally perforated with holes like a Swiss cheese.

Although Chester Gould tired of the constant parody of his beloved Tracy, the appearance of Fosdick in the highly popular Li'l Abner strip continuously reinforced Tracy's own popularity.

Al Capp wasn't the only cartoonist to parody Dick Tracy. Not surprisingly the crew at MAD magazine had their fun with Tracy several times.

Chester Gould was an extraordinary cartoonist. He had the conviction he would succeed and he did. But he never forgot the functions of the comics, which in his opinion were to entertain and to sell the next day's newspaper.

"Old Granite Jaw," Ed Sullivan, received a special portrait by Gould when Gould appeared on his popular nationally televised variety show in the 1950's.

Dick Tracy and I

by Chester Gould

Prior to my retirement from the strip in late December 1977, I'd written and drawn Dick Tracy for 46 years, two months and 21 days, so I guess I know the guy.

I'm often asked where I got the idea for Tracy's face, the square chin and hook nose. Well, in drawing the character, it had been my idea to picture him as a modern Sherlock Holmes, if Holmes were a young man living today, dressed as a modern G-man and bearing the traditional characteristics.

My production of Dick Tracy was mostly a case of constant application and continuous effort. Of course any work you like is not really hard work—it's a happy operation. Cartooning is one of the most rewarding businesses in the world because all of the thinking and physical effort you put into production of a strip results in something concrete that's right there for readers to see in black and white.

Of necessity, gunplay is part of the Dick Tracy strip, and was from the very beginning. That's natural. The law is always armed. Back in 1931 no cartoon had ever shown a detective character fighting it out face to face with crooks via the hot lead route. This detail brought certain expressions of misgiving from newspapers that were prospective Tracy customers. However, within two years this sentiment had faded to the point where six other strips of a similar pattern were on the market and the gunplay bogey had faded into thin air.

There is also more humor in Dick Tracy than many people seem to realize. Humor doesn't have to be jokes and gags. B.O. Plenty came into my strip in 1945 as the image of pioneer characters I knew in Oklahoma as a boy. My own grandfather looked a lot like B.O. Plenty in terms of his whiskers. He was a farmer. He'd let his hair and whiskers grow all winter. Then he'd visit town in the spring and have my dad cut his hair. You'd hardly know him after the transformation. A fellow like B.O. Plenty is uneducated but smart, cunning

and tough with a ready, built-in funny bone. The incongruity of the rough exterior with these subtle qualities is humor in its richest form.

I've tried very hard to use that subtle formula throughout Dick Tracy. Serious writing must be seasoned with humor to be complete. The excruciating suspense of a mystery story is enhanced by the nervous laugh and quip of a finale that says, "All's well." If Dick Tracy's success had a secret ingredient during my years as pilot, I like to believe it was this.

My schedule on Dick Tracy was pleasantly rigid and I liked it that way. I did most of my writing on Friday and Monday, did a Sunday on Tuesday, then two or three dailies on Wednesday and three more on Thursday. Sometimes I'd spend time on Friday checking on the mistakes I made earlier in the week. I remember drawing a Sunday page that showed a hoodlum standing in the background, in a doorway, all through the page. Not until the strip got into print did anyone notice that this guy had on four different hats as he stood in that doorway. I found if you can keep to a schedule, you can make yourself available, when needed, to your family.

The strip was drawn on 3-ply Strathmore and I used a Gillot 290 pen point. The 290 is more flexible than the 170 pen point which I know many cartoonists use. However, I always wanted to get a swing to my line. I did a lot of brush work and used a Windsor-Newton #4 brush. To me it seemed not too heavy and not too fine.

Underneath the ink of course was some very detailed pencilling with a medium weight pencil that was hard enough not to make an impossible smudge from contact with my hand. I also prefered to use a long red eraser called a Pink Lady rather than art gum erasers, which I used just to clean up the whole strip after I'd finished with it. I liked how the Pink Lady would let me get into small areas to change details. Higgins black ink was also what I preferred.

I always thought of Tracy as being just

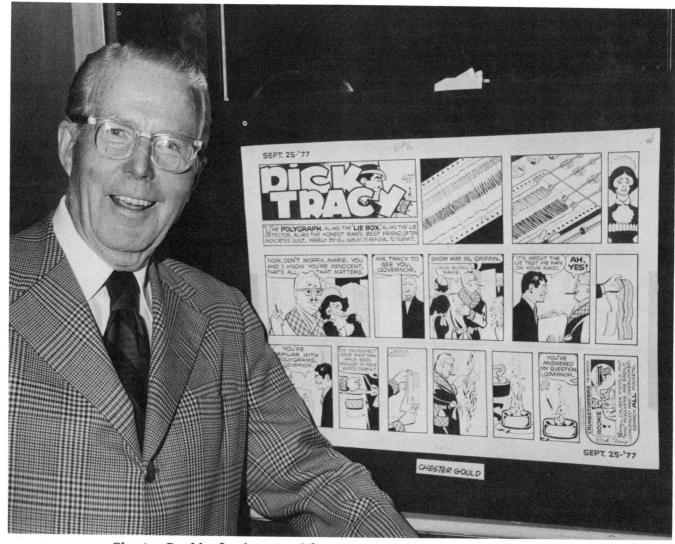

Chester Gould, after he retired from writing and drawing Dick Tracy, made several appearances at the Chicago Comics Convention. The original behind him is from the last Tracy story he worked on and is reproduced in this volume. (Photo courtesy of Rich Pietrzyk.)

about six feet tall and an ordinary guy with a good build on him.

Maybe I should mention that I've always been a guy who liked to get up early. Often on a Saturday morning I'd be up by three in the morning and would sit down and try to write the week's strip and break it up with answering fan mail. Every Monday morning I would commute into my office at the *Chicago Tribune* tower and begin pencilling. Psychologically it was a big lift for me to have to travel into my office in Chicago every Monday. It broke up my pattern of being at home in Woodstock. I took the early train that brought me into the Chicago station at 7:30 a.m. My office was on the 26th floor of the tower.

All you have in the cartoon business is time and it is important not to waste your time. While working on Dick Tracy the furthest I ever got ahead of deadline was 14 weeks. However, our normal deadline was 11 weeks so I only had a three-week fudge factor. The only time I ever used those three weeks was a time my wife Edna and I visited London for two weeks and then New York City for one week. That was the longest vacation I'd ever taken up to that time.

Daily strips, because you don't have the color separations and engraving to consider, were on a six-week deadline.

With my stories I always tried to have two highpoints per week. Usually one appeared in the dailies between Thursday and Saturday and the final highpoint would appear in the Sunday. One thing I did that I think was helpful and kept readership was to try to have at least one panel in every daily that the readers felt they had to investigate; something that would appeal to the eye for just a second so they would take a second look.

Often I would use a detail of an everyday object that fitted into the story to contrast with, say, Tracy's profile in the panel before. Then you might jump off to a long shot to move the reader's eye into a completely different perspective.

I liked to show the latest architecture in the strip to create what some have referred to as "urban landscapes." As part of this I got on to a system of drawing inverted V's and totally simplified the process.

Layout is just as important in a comic strip as it is in an advertisement. You have to grab the reader's attention and that's what I tried to do with my layouts. I gave my solid black ink areas a lot of thought. They

Gould's ability to conjure up the bizaare even invaded the humorous moments in Dick Tracy. Here Tracy in the hospital rewards his friends, the singing group The Gallstones, with some souvenir real gallstones. No cartoonists can draw day after day without a goof; note that in the first daily the female singer miraculously changes outfits between verses.

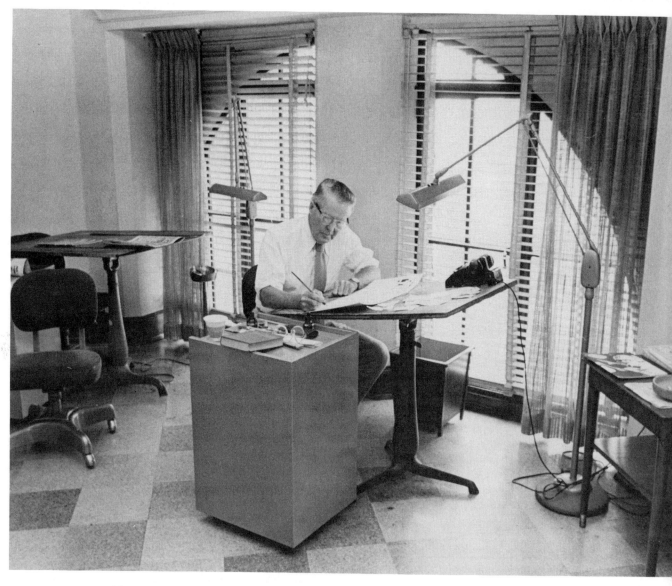

Chester Gould at work in his Tribune Tower studio in Chicago in the 1960's.

were no accident. The black areas were used to direct the reader's eye; you might say they acted as arrows.

Of course one of my so-called trademarks was to use little boxes with an arrow and a label such as "wrist radio" to be sure nobody missed what I was trying to show them. Average reading time of a comic strip is under 30 seconds and I wanted these busy people to take note of certain things. In fact, in the case of the two-way wrist radio I just about always used an arrow. The reason being I wanted the reader for ever and ever to remember that when the first two-way wrist radio comes into reality, and it's not here yet, that he saw the first one in Dick Tracy.

I must admit I'm not conscious of any intent on my part to modify my style of artwork over the years, but nothing is static, especially in art. What I strived to do in all my years on the strip was to make something quick and easy to read. But I constantly work to make my artwork look distinctive from anybody else's.

There's a very strong religious overtone that runs throughout Tracy. I make my characters pray to the Almighty when all else fails. Anybody who is offended by prayer and the Bible, I want them to be offended. My faith in God and in my Bible and my religious background is very important to me.

Without being critical of my peers and

Within the illustration:

STREAMLINED
~~RS~~ HAVE NOTHING ON US!

~~I~~'VE BEEN SHOOTING ~~TH~~ROUGH **DETROIT** VIA THE ~~FR~~EE PRESS FOR YEARS!

WISH I WAS OUT OF JAIL AND HAD A NEW CAR.

To the Free Press and our readers in Detroit— with best wishes

CHESTER GOULD

Chester Gould was never too busy to promote Dick Tracy or thank his readers for their support. This special drawing by Gould was used frequently in papers around the country to accompany any article on him as Dick Tracy's creator. And Gould would always sign a personal message.

cartoonists who are personal friends, I think I can say that this trying to please everybody, the public as a whole, gives you a strip with nothing in it. And I think the general trend to insipidness has lost readers.

During the 1960's many people referred to some of my work with Dick Tracy as science-fiction when I introduced the magnetic space coupe, the air car, Moon Maid, and the people from the moon. That was not science-fiction. I am not a science-fiction writer. I was basing everything I did on what was being done by NASA, and they were making a lot of noise and doing nothing. So I researched the moon, its extreme heat and extreme cold, etc., and took things from there with my imagination.

Sure I had gangsters in space. I had this one guy in the story taken for a ride and just floated out into space. That's the way it will be. I'm convinced as soon as they've established valuable minerals that can be mined in space, there will be gangsterism in space.

I irritated NASA a great deal because I brought out things they will be doing in space one of these days.

If you just go along and don't raise a big

stink every so often with Dick Tracy, it means you're starting to go flat. My last real stink was when Tracy vaporized the villain Intro with a laser cannon. Somebody asks Tracy where Intro is and the response is, "You're breathing him."

However, I must repeat I never considered myself to be writing science-fiction. It's just that my vision of the future is just ahead of its time. I'm not one to live in the past. For example, I've always felt my favorite villain in Dick Tracy is the one I'm working on at the moment.

The Governor might be called my last villain but he wasn't really a villain, he was a crooked politician. In our era those guys are a dime a dozen. However, One of my most gruesome villains was Haf & Haf whom I created in 1966. I've always thought he was quite a character.

I tried for constant variety in all aspects of my strip, right down to what I put in both the foreground and background to support the main action. I tried to jazz it up all the time. If people didn't want to buy tomorrow's paper to see what was happening in Dick Tracy, I had failed in my goal.

I'm often asked what comic strips I read. Without any questions, as an adult, "Orphan Annie" while Harold Gray was at the

Pregnant, married just a year, and a murderess, Mrs. Z.Z. Welz is taken into custody for the killing of her husband, a lowlife and obsessive obscene phone caller. Note how Gould has the mother-to-be gaze at the phone as she says, "It's been a year of agony." Pregnant women were not common in the comics, and this episode was published in 1975.

height of his abilities was my favorite. I admired both Harold's writing and drawing. He had a rather simple style of drawing but when he wanted to draw a mansion of some triple millionaire with a chauffeured car in front, nobody could put the feeling over any better than Harold Gray. We used to talk quite a bit and he was a great guy. Gray was a man of great conviction.

In my estimation television and a liberal view on comic strips by editors has delegated all the controversy and conviction to the news end of the business and to columnists, the editorial side. That side has lots of character, but they don't want to be bothered with comic strips. The result is that they've castrated most comic strips from any convictions and turned out a bunch of milk-sop strips. In contrast, the old newspaper kings that built publishing empires in this country were people of conviction.

Another strip that I think is very funny is "Snuffy Smith." It used to be called "Barney Google." As a kid I loved "Mutt and Jeff." My father used to buy the Oklahoma City *Daily Oklahoman* just so I could read it. It was my love of that comic strip which made me decide to become a cartoonist.

There's no doubt the good Lord or somebody looked after Gould. I worked for Hearst for five and a half years in Chicago as a cartoonist, but I gave the job up because they had me stymied. They were having me do strips that were imitations of other strips. I did one called "Fillum Fables," which was an imitation of Ed Whelan's "Minute Movies." So I resigned and was confident I could get some kind of work, as my original work in Chicago had

been in commercial art. That's how I got into the art department of the Chicago *Daily News.* This was in 1929. The Depression hadn't come on but it was just getting ready to. I was married and had a family and my pay went from about $100 a week down to $50 per week. But we got along.

Along about May 1931, I came up with the idea for "Plainclothes Tracy." I knew Captain Patterson of the Chicago *Tribune* had rejected everything I'd sent him for ten years. So I said to myself the heck with it, I'm going to submit one that I like. It had this one fellow tied up and the villain was going to have a blow torch put to him to make him talk. Then Tracy shows up and saves him.

When Patterson made up his mind it was all ahead full steam. I had four weeks' work on Dick Tracy including Sunday pages in less than two weeks time. I never slept. But Captain Patterson knew what would sell newspapers.

It may shock fans of Dick Tracy, but while I was working on the strip I actually tried to block out of my mind the past villains that I created. That way you can concentrate your creative energy on thinking up new things. I think the best story in the world is one where the writer doesn't know how it's going to end when he starts it. I used to deliberately get Dick Tracy into impossible situations. Then I'd let the drama of the situation simmer for a week. I'd use this as a challenge to myself. If you do things the easy way you get a nothing as a result. That's why I like to write my stories only a week at a time and then draw them, rather than planning weeks in advance.

THE BATTLE IN THE BARN! LIZZ, WHO WAS CONSIDERED DEAD, DRAWS A HIDDEN DERRINGER, AND—

ONE, TWO,

Reg. U.S. Pat. Off.: © 1962 by The Chicago Tribune.

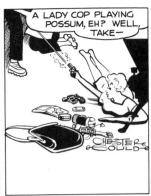

THE BULLET MISSES ITS MARK, BUT IT DETERS THE GUNMAN FROM KILLING AUNTIE.

A LADY COP PLAYING POSSUM, EH? WELL, TAKE—

CHESTER GOULD

THE SECOND AND ONLY REMAINING SHOT IN THE DERRINGER FINDS ITS MARK.

HONEST JOHN HOEDY, OWNER OF THE GENERAL STORE! HOW COULD YOU?

HER GUN WON'T HELP YOU, IT HAS NO BULLETS.

BUT, ALAS, WHILE AUNTIE KNEELS ON THE FLOOR, THE CARTRIDGES FROM LIZZ'S GUN HAVE SPILLED FROM HER APRON POCKET.

Reg. U.S. Pat. Off.: © 1962 by The Chicago Tribune.

THE DERRINGER SHOTS SPENT, LIZZ HAS BUT ONE WEAPON LEFT—A KARATE BLOW TO THE BACK OF THE NECK.

NO!

CHESTER GOULD

OKAY—CUT IT!

TRACY! SAM!

Reg. U.S. Pat. Off.: © 1962 by The Chicago Tribune.

SAM AND I SUSPECTED THINGS WOULD HAPPEN— WHEN YOU RADIOED AT 3 A.M. YOU HAD DISCOVERED AUNTIE'S HIDING PLACE. WE PARKED JUST 2 MILES DOWN THE ROAD.

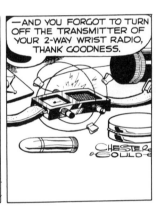

—AND YOU FORGOT TO TURN OFF THE TRANSMITTER OF YOUR 2-WAY WRIST RADIO, THANK GOODNESS.

CHESTER GOULD

HE'S HONEST JOHN HOEDY WHO RUNS THE GENERAL STORE.

WHO IS THAT?

MY NEPHEW.

JOHN, WHAT'S HAPPENED TO YOU? YOU WERE GOING TO LET HIM KILL ME?

CHESTER GOULD

WE'LL WANT THE EXAMINER AND AN AMBULANCE.

IT'S THE SAME OLD STORY— EASY BUCKS.

2-WAY WRIST RADIO

In the mid-1950's Gould introduced a female newspaper photographer, Lizz, who soon joined the force as a rookie. She has developed into one of the strongest female characters in syndicated comics. In this 1962 shootout, Lizz proves she's nobody to mess around with. While her hairstyle and color changes, Lizz's trademark has always been her distinctive eye makeup.

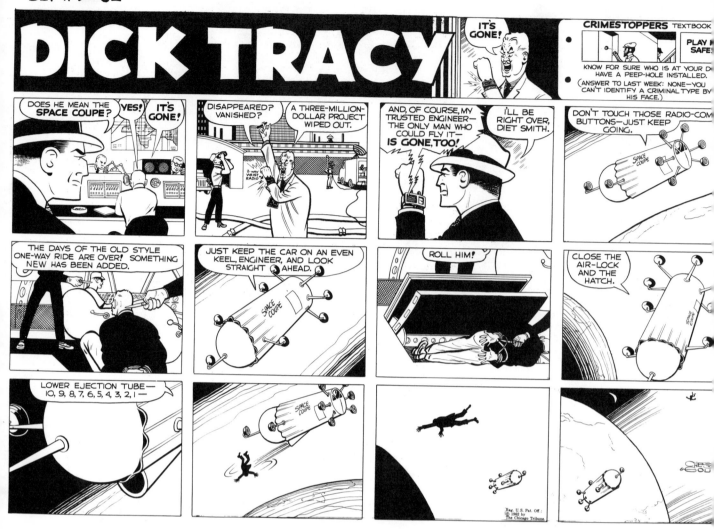

Less than a month after the Space Coupe's debut, the first gangland-style rubout takes place in space. Gould didn't ease into his so-called "Moon Period"; he jumped in completely. Some critics argue that Tracy was better strictly as an earthbound detective.

I used to be a fanatic about doing my own color key charts for the Sunday pages for years. I think I turned that job over to Rick Fletcher about 1970. However, after many years I found out that the color charts we made meant so damn little. The engraving rooms got to doing the comics in the cheapest possible way. In the old days the *New York News* and the *Chicago Tribune* used to publish Dick Tracy Sundays in exactly the colors I'd done. I always made great use of red, yellow, blue and green. And I tried to do away entirely with browns, orange and purple.

I always used to hand deliver the week's worth of Tracy when I went into the office on Monday, right to the mailing cage in the Tribune Tower. In later years Rick Fletcher would do that while I would be starting my pencilling. Also, before I turned in my work I always had three sets of photostats made in case anything was lost by the syndicate. That was before Xerox machines.

For me, Dick Tracy has been one continuous detective story. I don't break it down into different periods as many of my fans do. Also I made a point of not reading any of the modern detective novels. I was of course a big fan of Sherlock Holmes. And I did read and reread the Sherlock Holmes stories. I always found some inspiration in them. The Sherlock Holmes stories weren't like Dick Tracy but they always had that element of suspense in them. Sir Arthur Conan Doyle is the grandfather of the classic suspense story, any kind of true suspense story, in my opinion. I also considered myself a disciple of Edgar Allan

The writ of habeas corpus results in "The Doll," one of the ten most wanted, getting out on bail on a hit-and-run charge. Gould strove to show what he thought were both the strengths and weaknesses in the court system from the point of view of the police. The Doll's accomplice demonstrates how evil Gould's villains can be. Poisoning a blind girl's seeing eye dog is about as low as a hood can get. The dog was modeled after Gould's own pet.

SPARKLE WALKS HER TO THE EYE DOCTOR ON SATURDAYS.

THEY PASS THIS CORNER AT APPROXIMATELY 10:20 A.M. WITH THE DOG.

GET ME A POUND OF HAMBURGER MEAT.

AND RENT ME A SANTA CLAUS SUIT.

"WHA'D'E SAY?"

"REPEAT THAT, PLEASE."

HOW DO I LOOK?

Do Your CHRISTMAS SHOPPING EARLIER at RIX

NOW LET ME HAVE A BAG OF THOSE MEATBALLS.

OH, I DON'T LIKE THIS.

OH, I CAN'T GO FOR THIS. I'M A LITTLE SICK ALREADY.

POISONED MEAT! A BLIND GIRL'S DOG!

HE'S GONE NUTS. I OUGHT TO DRILL HIM.

AS TINKY AND STONY WAIT AT THE CORNER WHERE THEY ARE TO MEET SPARKLE—

U.S. MAIL

RAINED NEVER TO ACCEPT FOOD FROM STRANGERS, CAN STONY RESIST THIS FRESH GROUND MEAT?

YOUR DOG SEEMS TO BE ILL, LITTLE GIRL.

MY POOR, DEAR STONY! WHAT COULD—

—OH, SPARKLE, THANK HEAVEN YOU'RE HERE.

I'M A VETERINARIAN, MA'AM JUST HAPPENED BY. MY HOSPITAL'S IN THE NEXT BLOCK.

THIS IS TERRIBLE, TINKY, BUT WE'RE DUE AT THE EYE DOCTOR—

WHAT SHALL WE DO?

Poe. As a kid I had been a fan of the Tom Swift stories, which also were always based on danger and menace.

Through the years I never had the urge to actually write mystery novels, as I've always felt the comic strip format was my forte.

Dick Tracy also has a unique place in the field of so-called serious art. I was rather complimented when Andy Warhol used this comic strip character that I had created. He didn't draw that well but that wasn't his forte. I just considered Warhol's painting as more publicity for Dick Tracy.

The other very famous representation of Tracy was by Al Capp in 'Li'l Abner." Capp wrote me, in fact, and asked my permission to parody Dick Tracy. At the time he was doing a lot of one-shot things in the strip and I figured what the heck. But with "Fearless Fosdick," Capp continued to use and use the character. I met Capp three or four years after he came up with "Fearless Fosdick" at one of the April conventions of the National Cartoonists Society. Everything was fine and congenial and he asked me when I was going to do a takeoff of "Li'l Abner," but I explained I wished I could but that I couldn't adapt my stuff like he did his. I only saw Capp one time after that, again at an April NCS dinner, and the first thing he said was, "When are you going to do 'Li'l Abner'?" I think he really expected I would pick up on it, but I said to myself I will never parody another strip in Dick Tracy. Also I think the public very quickly becomes extremely bored with any little feud between writers or cartoonists and I wanted nothing to do with anything like that.

JAN. 29-'76

FEB. 2-'76

A computer search for a suspect contrasts with Lizz's looking through Tracy's rogues' gallery. Lispy led a gang of women bank robbers. She led the group with an iron hand, and a transgressor is seen doing punishment pushups in just her bra and panties with a ten-pound weight on her back.

DICK TRACY
DETECTIVE

The front and back cover of the first Dick Tracy promotion issued by the Chicago Tribune Newspapers Syndicate. The piece featured two Sundays reproduced in color on the inside, and on the back a sales letter dated December 17, 1931, barely two months after the start of the strip.

Every kid wants to be a detective and wear a tin star. The same instinct for adventure and action is carried over to adult life. Evidence the unprecedented popularity of mystery stories and detective fiction. All the years have not dimmed the light of Sherlock Holmes. To satisfy this interest among the readers of your paper, you should know about Tracy, newest Chicago Tribune comic strip character.

Dick Tracy is a plainclothes man, a member of the police department. He is the prototype of the present hero—but on the *positive* side. An antidote to maudlin sympathy with society's enemies, he creates no glamour for the underworld. Children love this character, and parents and teachers approve of him.

Created by Chester Gould, amateur criminologist as well as versatile artist, Dick Tracy is a daily detective story in graphic form. It parallels in interest your front page stories. It has action, character and humor, love interest—and continuity—an all-around all-age appeal! The daily strips are serial in content. The Sunday pages are complete episodes.

This strip is now four months old. It is running in the New York News. New York is admittedly the hardest and most competitive circulation market in the country. The News, with the largest circulation in America, finds it difficult to do anything new in the circulation way. Yet J. S. Sullivan, circulation manager, says that Dick Tracy caused more favorable comment than anything The News has ever used; and as a Sunday feature brought in immediate increases! See his letter on the back page.

We can furnish this Sunday feature in one-half page or in tabloid size. Daily strip—5 columns.

WIRE, write or phone for territories still open!

220 East 42d Street, New York City   Tribune Tower, Chicago

CHICAGO TRIBUNE NEWSPAPERS SYNDICATE

Three daily strips of Dick Tracy and a letter from Mr. J. S. Sullivan, New York News, who writes: " . . . going over big in New York . . . have heard more favorable comment on this strip than on anything we ever used! . . . "

CHICAGO TRIBUNE NEWSPAPERS SYNDICATE
News Building, New York ● Tribune Tower, Chicago

The First 12 Days of Dick Tracy Daily Strips

GOOD EVENING, MR. TRUEHEART — HOW'S THE DELICATESSEN BUSINESS THIS EVENING?

WELL! HELLO, DICK — IF YOU'D BEEN A MINUTE LATER YOU'D HAVE HAD TO GO UPSTAIRS BY THE SIDE ENTRANCE — I WAS JUST CLOSING UP FOR SUPPER.

(Copyright: 1931 By News Syndicate Co., Inc.)

HELLO TESS — GEE, YOU LOOK PRETTY

WELL WHY NOT FOR MY VERY BESTEST BOY FRIEND — HURRY UP. YOU POOR DEARS, WE'RE ALL STARVED

MAMMA, THE BREADEATERS ARE ALL HERE — HOW'S THE FOOD?

OH, AND AM I GLAD YOU'VE COME! IT'LL GET ME AWAY FROM THIS PAPER AND THESE TALES ABOUT GANGSTERS I CAN'T BEAR TO READ THEM AND I CAN'T LEAVE THEM ALONE.

CONTINUED

GEE, MRS. TRUEHEART, IT WAS A WONDERFUL MEAL! DANG IT — I'VE GAINED FIVE POUNDS SINCE TESS HAS BEEN HAVING ME OUT HERE FOR YOUR SUPPERS — NO KIDDING.

RAVE ON, BIG BOY!

GO ON WITH YOU, DICK.

(Copyright: 1931 By News Syndicate Co., Inc.)

LET 'EM DO THE DISHES IF THEY WANT TO! — BY THE GREAT SAINTS AIN'T YOU HAD ENOUGH DISH WASHING AFTER TWENTY YEARS, MAMMA?

OH I KNOW, BUT —

TESS DARLING, I'VE GOT SOMETHING DARNED IMPORTANT I WANT TO TELL YOU TONIGHT.

AND I'M SO ANXIOUS TO HEAR IT, DICK.

WHILE IN AN ALLEY ACROSS THE STREET FROM THE DELICATESSEN STAND TWO STRANGE AND SINISTER FORMS —

YEAH — DAT'S TH' PLACE, CRUTCH. HE KEEPS HIS SAVINGS ON THE SECOND FLOOR IN A BOX — DE BIG BOY SAYS IT'S A CINCH.

A CINCH, EH?

EMIL TRUEHEART DELICATESSEN

CONTINUED

— NINE HUNDRED EIGHTY — NINE HUNDRED NINETY — ONE THOUSAND — AN EVEN THOUSAND DOLLARS! — AND WE DON'T OWE A SOUL, MAMMA!

I'M SO PROUD OF YOU, EMIL

(Copyright: 1931 By News Syndicate Co., Inc.)

YOU SHOULD HAVE SEEN OLD BANKER JEDD'S EYES WHEN I PAID OFF THAT MORTGAGE YESTERDAY — HE SAYS, "TRUEHEART, IT'S A PLEASURE TO DO BUSINESS WITH YOU."

SAY, WILL YOU TWO COME OUT HERE? DICK AND I HAVE SOMETHING REAL IMPORTANT TO TELL YOU.

TESS, I'M THE HAPPIEST MAN IN THE WORLD TONIGHT.

AND ON A ROOF NOT FAR AWAY TWO SHADOWY FORMS CONTINUE THEIR EVIL VIGIL.

HM — LOOKS LIKE HE'S PUTTIN' DE DOUGH IN A BOX UNDER THE BED — OH HO — THIS JOB'LL BE A SET-UP, CRUTCH.

OH YEAH?

MR. TRUEHEART, TESS AND I HAVE DECIDED TO GET MARRIED — I KNOW I HAVEN'T HAD THE BREAKS AS FAR AS MONEY'S CONCERNED — BUT WITH HER BY MY SIDE I'LL FIND A WAY.

OF COURSE YOU'LL FIND A WAY, MY BOY — AND CONGRATULATIONS TO BOTH OF YOU. I'VE GOT FAITH IN YOU, DICK.

CAN'T WE DO SOMETHING TO CELEBRATE OUR HAPPINESS? YOU TWO ARE OUT OF DEBT AND WE'RE ENGAGED.

STICK 'EM UP — ALLA Y'U

AND KEEP 'EM UP! WE'RE AFTER THAT DOUGH — WHERE IS IT?

(Copyright: 1931 By News Syndicate Co., Inc.)

Panel 1: IT WAS A HOLD-UP, CHIEF, A NASTY JOB. THEY'VE KIDNAPPED A GIRL AND MURDERED HER FATHER — AND WE JUST SENT HER MOTHER TO THE HOSPITAL PROSTRATE FROM SHOCK.

Panel 2: TOO BAD! — THE OLD DUCK DIDN'T HAVE A CHANCE — NOT A CHANCE! THEY NEVER DO WHEN ONE OF THE "BIG BOYS" RATS STRIKE.

Panel 3: BUT THE GIRL — THEY TOOK HER — WHY DO WE STAND HERE LIKE IDIOTS? — WE MUST SAVE HER!

TRY TO BE SANE MAN — THEY'VE GOT HER MILES AWAY FROM HERE BY NOW — WE'LL HAVE TO FIGURE THIS THING OUT.

Panel 4: OVER THE BODY OF YOUR FATHER, TESS, I SWEAR I'LL FIND YOU AND AVENGE THIS THING — I SWEAR IT —

Panel 5: TESS TRUEHEART WAS MY FIANCEE — JUST BEFORE THE STICK-UP WE'D BEEN TELLING OUR PARENTS OF OUR PLANS.

Panel 6: YOU SAY THE OLD MAN HAD ABOUT A THOUSAND BUCKS IN HIS BEDROOM SAFE. — IT'S FUNNY HE DIDN'T PATRONIZE THE BANKS.

NOT AT ALL. HE'D LOST OVER FIVE HUNDRED DOLLARS IN THE LAST YEAR IN SMALL BANK FAILURES.

Panel 7: YEAH, MILLIGAN, THIS IS THE CHIEF — WHAT ? YOU SAY THEY'VE PICKED UP THE GIRL'S TRAIL?

Panel 8: TRACY — HOW'D YOU LIKE TO JOIN THE PLAIN CLOTHES SQUAD? I THINK YOU'D BE A BIG HELP IN FINDING TESS TRUEHEART AND CATCHING HER FATHER'S MURDERER.

CHIEF YOU'VE TAKEN THE WORDS RIGHT OUT OF MY MOUTH.

Panel 9: NOW A MEMBER OF THE PLAIN-CLOTHES SQUAD, DICK TRACY PREPARES TO LEAD THE POLICE DRAG NET IN SEARCH OF HIS KIDNAPPED SWEETHEART, TESS, AND THE GANG THAT MURDERED HER FATHER — BUT FIRST HE CALLS AT THE HOSPITAL WHERE TESS' MOTHER LIES PROSTRATED FROM GRIEF AND SHOCK.

HER CONDITION IS QUITE SERIOUS, MR. TRACY.

Panel 10: HERE, TESS DARLING, MY BABY — PUT YOUR HEAD HERE ON MAMMA'S SHOULDER — LOOK FATHER AT THOSE CURLS —

Panel 11: I CAN'T BEAR IT — IT'S TOO MUCH —

Panel 12: MEANWHILE, SOMEWHERE IN THE HEART OF GANGLAND IN A DARKENED, GUARDED ROOM —

WHERE AM I AND WHAT ARE THEY GOING TO DO WITH ME?

NOW, NOW — JUST DRINK THIS TEA — I THINK YOU'RE GOING TO HAVE CALLERS PRETTY SOON.

Panel 13: THAT'S THE GIRL, BOSS.

UNTIE 'ER — LET 'ER STAND UP.

Panel 14: KINDA PRETTY AINTCHA, SISTER? — CUTE KID —

SMACK

Panel 15: SO YOU AINT SWINGING WITH "BIG BOY", EH GIRLIE? TIE 'ER UP CRUTCH — WE'LL LET 'ER CURE A COUPLE OF MORE DAYS — THEN WE CAN TALK TO 'ER.

Panel 16: WHERE EVER THE GIRL IS THERE'S A CHANCE FOR HER IF SHE DON'T LOSE HER SPUNK.

SPUNK — HA! SHE'S GOT MORE SPUNK THAN A HALF DOZEN OF YOU FLAT FEET! — STEP ON IT GILLIGAN.

(Copyright: 1931: By News Syndicate Co., Inc.)

At the request of LIFE magazine in 1944, Gould drew this special depiction of his hero and his villains. This was at the point that Gould's villains were becoming as much his trademark as Tracy's profile. They are (front, left to right) The Brow, The Mole, Pruneface, Flattop, Mrs. Pruneface, Littleface, Mama and the Midget; (rear) B-B Eyes (with cigar), faceless Redrum, and 88 Keyes. In a self-caricature, Gould kneels lower right, ready to defend Tracy with his art gum eraser if need be.

The creation of the two-way wrist TV actually gave Chester Gould more dramatic visual effects than he'd been able to use with the two-way wrist radio. In this sequence, Tracy has a close call in a burning truck. Gould's highly sylized drawing of fire is especially effective. This episode occurred during the "Moon period" of Gould's work, and the air cars are used to assist in spreading foam to extinguish the fire.

Dick Tracy's daddy fires some practice rounds at his 130-acre farm in Woodstock, Illinois, northwest of Chicago.

In order to excel, you have to funnel your own energies into what you are doing, to make it the best possible, and the hell with what other people do.

For a little over 46 years I made a point to cut the side issues down to a bare minimum so I could concentrate on producing Dick Tracy. And I sort of got a reputation for being a loner. However, for many years there was a very congenial group of cartoonists here in Chicago and we'd meet for lunch or whatever.

Over the years I think Dick Tracy has gotten his fair share of publicity and much of the reason is people either love the strip or hate it. If your strip is lukewarm, nobody talks about you. That's not the way to keep a comic strip in the limelight.

The best advice I can give the fellows who are carrying on Dick Tracy is that yesterday's comic strip is dead as a mackerel. The strip to worry about is the one for tomorrow. That has always been my approach to keeping Dick Tracy interesting to the reader.

Death in the City

by Maurice Horn

When Dick Tracy first appeared, the adventure strip, as an accepted genre, was little more than two years old. While antecedents, including "Wash Tubbs," go back to the early years of the century, it was only in 1929 that "Tarzan" and "Buck Rogers" firmly established the action heroes on the newspaper pages, alongside the host of cheeky kids, flirtatious young girls and henpecked husbands that had hitherto been the staple of the medium.

While "Buck Rogers" and "Tarzan" both owed their inspiration to previously published novels, Dick Tracy from its inception came out as the fully-formed creation of a single author—Chester Gould. This fact is important: from its very first, still awkwardly told story, Gould had to carry the full artistic and narrative freight of the strip without the help of an already existing framework. Having no precedent or model to fall back, on Gould had to create his own conventions: this he did—masterfully, and the development of Chet Gould as an *auteur* is as fascinating to follow as the parallel development of Dick Tracy as a comic strip.

The comic pages of the newspapers of the early thirties may have been bereft of direct inspiration for Gould, but not so the news pages: indeed the headlines and stories about the gangster wars and the pervasive corruption that Prohibition had engendered proved the immediate cause of Gould's slowly crystallizing theme—that of ruthless crime and inescapable punishment. Moral outrage has long been a source for artistic expression, but expression has to match conviction—in strength, in clarity, in forthrightness—for it to become all-persuasive (not every Sunday preacher is a Milton). Here, I believe, lies Chester Gould's greatest accomplishment: he made Dick Tracy into the vehicle of a unified thought and a single vision.

Nothing happens in a vacuum: Tracy does not take place in some future century or some distant jungle, but here and now. This choice in itself is proof to the fact that Gould was aware of the social and cultural currents swirling all around him. In a 1970 interview Gould averred that he had been influenced most of all by the Sherlock Holmes stories (and there is indeed more than a passing physiognomical resemblance between the Baker Street detective and Gould's plainclothes cop) and by Poe's tales of detection (which may account for Gould's delight in procedural and laboratory minutiae).

In that same interview Gould brushed aside any inference that either the contemporary pulps or the novels of Dashiell Hammett may have had any influence in the creation or development of his detective strip; yet Tracy often appears as the very distillate of the "bloody pulps" (with the blood flowing red on Sundays). Since Gould and the pulp and mystery writers used the same raw material taken from the same newspapers and the same incidents, it can easily be concluded that they shared a common perception about the decaying social order of the times—the peculiar *Zeitgeist* of Prohibition-era America. Along with the Depression, urban crime was the specter that haunted America: writing about the hard-boiled school of detective fiction (but this may also apply to Tracy) Raymond Chandler spoke of "the smell of fear which these stories managed to generate." Death in the city, death *and* the city became the pervasive imagery of menace (and still so remains to this day). The characters in these dark parables "lived in a world gone wrong," to quote Chandler again, "a world in which . . . civilization had created the machinery for its own destruction. . . ." For moral and social balance the myth of the city gone mad necessitated the counter-myth of the shining hero going down to do battle with the forces of evil into the very heart of the urban darkness—the obligatory descent into hell. Whether consciously or not Chester Gould put Tracy alongside the Continental Op, Sam Spade, and, later, Phil Marlowe in the ranks of the new order of modern knights who, from

Gould's skill at depicting the menace of the urban setting--its back alleys, hardedges, black ominous contrasts between light and dark--are, according to Maurice Horn, among the strengths of the strip. This Sunday page has all these elements.

inner compulsion or moral revulsion, "down these mean streets must go."

Gould found his theme first and evolved a graphic style to fit this theme only second. He was too shrewd an artist to rely on the old stand-bys, such as "Mutt and Jeff," on which he had grown up, although there is a certain "cartooniness" to Tracy, especially in the early days. Conversely the painstaking draftsmanship of an Harold Foster couldn't possibly fit his purpose: no code of chivalry existed down where Tracy lived and worked, and the code of the streets did not call for elegance of line or gracefulness of gesture. Gould's renderings were black, ominous, his line sharp and nervous, the perspective compact, opressive. His imagery Gould took directly from news photos, complete with sharply-edged contours and flattened backgrounds, photoprints of the city's soul,

with its skyscapes, its back alleys, its gaudy neon signs, its grandeur and squalor.

The mastery of Gould's tales resides most of all in their telling. From the silent movies of his youth (which he had lovingly spoofed in his earlier "Fillum Fables") Gould borrowed relatively little: a certain fondness for medium and close shots, an exaggeration of pose, and a few archetypal faces (Tess Truehart first comes out as a cross between Mary Pickford and Lilian Gish). Once the talkies had gotten over their growing pains, their visual and verbal pacing proved much more influential on Gould: his daily strips and Sunday pages were soon to acquire the rhythmic quality that stamps Tracy's unique narrative mode. Duplicating the abstract space of the movie screen, each panel alternates close ups, long shots, angle views, etc., in quick succession, forcing a feeling of irresistible motion forward upon the reader. It should be noted that Gould's technique here is kinetic, but not strictly cinematic: it is not so much a transposition of movie filming and editing as an adaptation of camera movement to paper. The action pulses relentlessly ahead, it evokes the brutal unspooling of a newsreel rather than the smooth flow of a Hollywood picture.

For the almost fifty years that Chester Gould worked on Dick Tracy his influence grew steadily stronger, and it did not cease even after the strip had passed into other hands. Gould introduced the themes of violence, suspense, tension and terror into the comics. Soon after Tracy's initial success, rival syndicates brought out police strips with the avowed aim of beating Gould at his own game. In 1933 and 1934 alone there were more than a half-dozen, with, in the forefront, "Secret Agent X-9," "Red Barry" and "Dan Dunn" (this last one an out-and-out imitation of Gould's graphic and writing styles). While the best of the latter detective strips soon went their own way, they all owe a debt of gratitude to Tracy for the trails the strip had blazed during the first years of its existence.

Tracy's impact, however, extended well beyond the mystery genre into all areas of story strip writing. In many newspaper comics, juvenile themes gradually made place for adult themes (this is especially striking in the *New York News'* other great action strip of the time, "Terry and the Pirates"). The trend cannot be attributed solely to Gould, of course, but his famous detective had inarguably much to do with it, at least by example: in the 1940s Tracy-like plotlines found their way into such disparate strips as "Brick Bradford" and "Mary Worth" as vehicles for social realism beyond mere adventure or conventional soap-opera. The anti-comics crusade of the 1950s largely put an end to such developments: it is symptomatic that Dick Tracy is one of the few—the very few—story strips that survived unemasculated from this ordeal by fire (and censorship).

In his introduction to *The Celebrated Cases of Dick Tracy* (Chelsea House, 1970) Ellery Queen details all the contributions made by Tracy to the field of crime fiction. While one may quibble with some of his assumptions, he makes a strong case for Gould as a pioneer in the area of procedural fiction ("14 years ahead of Treat...24 years ahead of Marric...25 years ahead of McBain") as well as a major figure in the history of detective fiction.

Tracy is in fact an aggregate—or, better, a synthesis—of many strands in crime fiction. Integrating the puzzle elements of the traditional mystery tale, the violent action of the thriller, the atmospheric overtones of the suspense story, and the shock tatics of the pulps (with a dash of science-fiction thrown in), Gould's stories ultimately follow no tradition but triumphantly impose their own. As Gould himself succinctly put it: "I feel that Dick Tracy has set a pattern for much of the very excellent entertainment in crime detection and police work."

While Tracy could often be seen and heard in movies, on radio (and later on television), in the many adaptations that were made over the years, his longest shadow was cast on what came to be called *film noir.* The violent and gruesome deaths meted out by Gould to his fiendish criminals preceded the retributive endings of countless films, from Robert Siodmak's *The Dark Mirror* and *The Killers* to Fritz Lang's *The Big Heat,* while Gould's grotesque and psychopathic villains found their counterparts on the screen in such movies as *White Heat, Kiss of Death, Lady From Shanghai* and *Touch of Evil* (the last two by Orson Welles).

Tracy's influence extended all the way to Europe. With his usual flair for hyperbole, Federico Fellini once said of Tracy, "It's a hundred times more beautiful than the best American gangster films," and Alain Resnais, François Truffaut and others all have declared their admiration for Gould's creation. Even more revealing is Jean-Luc Godard's *Alphaville*, in which the use of shallow space, bleached-out backgrounds and contrasted lighting are all clearly derived from Tracy. For those who might still have missed the point, Eddie Constantine, the lead character, was made to look like Tracy, with his snap-brimmed fedora and beat-up trenchcoat.

Of course Dick Tracy has always been more than entertainment, and its more representative episodes bear closer resemblance to Bertolt Brecht's existential ambiguities about good and evil than Gould may be willing to admit. Tracy forms part of a typically twentieth-century intel-

Master of the macabre, Chester Gould often relied on the principle stated in the last panel: "Fate does funny things." Here the chase has come to an end with an ivy vine doing what the gallows couldn't.

lectual current that sees in the secular city a reflection of Dante's vision of hell as *la città dolente,* the city of pain. Thus on a higher plane does Chester Gould take his place in the cultural history of this century, a claim that few other cartoonists can make.

DICK TRACY

YES, TRACY, THIS TELEVISION ROOM IS A REAL KICK. IT'S LIKE GOING TO THE MOVIES.

THESE RECEIVERS PERMIT US TO WATCH ALL PARTS OF THE BUILDING AT ONE TIME—CELL BLOCKS, CORRIDORS, AND THE DESK.

THAT SECOND SCREEN SHOWS THE LITTLE OLD LADY WHO WAS FLASHING MIRROR SIGNALS TO BIG FROST. HER DAUGHTER IS BAILING HER OUT.

HER DAUGHTER?? SHE'S QUITE A NUMBER! YEAH. HEY—LET ME SEE THAT—

AHA! I'VE GOT TO **GET OUT IN THE HALL**—

HEY, **SLEET**! SLEET, BABY!

REMEMBER SAM CATCHEM FROM **BOSTON** TOWN? EH?

I—I NEVER SAW YOU BEFORE IN MY **LIFE**.

THEY DON'T CALL YOU **SLEET** FOR NOTHIN,' DO THEY, BABY? COME ON, DEFROST.

LISTEN, I'VE STILL GOT THE INFRARED PICTURE I TOOK OF YOU IN THAT DARK OFFICE TRYING TO RIFLE THE GOVERNOR'S BRIEF CASE—REMEMBER?

ALL RIGHT, YOU WIN, COPPER. GO TO THE CAB, MOTHER. I'LL SEE YOU AT THE APARTMENT.

I THOUGHT I WAS RID OF YOU WHEN I LEFT BOSTON.

I'M WORKING **HERE** NOW. FATE JUST WON'T KEEP US APART.

WHAT DO YOU WANT, COPPER? AND I HOPE YOU DROP DEAD TELLING ME.

NICE KID, AIN'T SHE, TRACY? LISTEN, I'VE GOT ENOUGH ON HER TO SEND HER UP FOR 20 YEARS. BUT SHE PLAYS BALL, SO I GO ALONG.

WHAT DO YOU **WANT**?

TAKE IT EASY, SLEET, EASY! WE WANT YOU TO HELP US LOCATE A COUPLE OF TORPEDOES WHO USED TO WORK FOR A GUY NAMED BIG FROST.

WHAT DO YOU THINK I AM? A **RADAR** SET?

HM? WEATHER REPORT: MUCH COLDER—WITH **SLEET**.

1-2-49

Reg. U.S. Pat. Off. Copyright, 1949, by The Chicago Tribune.

66

68

DICK TRACY

THERE—THE INSTALLATION OF THE TELEVISION CAMERA IS COMPLETE.

...URN ...ON, ...ACY.

HOW LONG WILL THE POWER ELEMENT LAST?

SEVENTY-TWO HOURS, SAM.

ALL RIGHT. NOW, YOU KNOW WHERE YOU'RE TO GO?

SURE—IT'S A CINCH—

I GO **WHEREVER SHE** GOES, AND I'M NOT TO LET HER SEE ME.

RIGHT—SCRAM.

...RACY, DO YOU AND ...AM REALLY TRUST ...HIS DAME, SLEET, TO HELP YOU LOCATE BIG FROST'S MEN?

CHIEF, I DON'T TRUST HER ANY FURTHER THAN I COULD TOSS A SQUAD CAR.

YEP, SHE SAID SHE HAD A DATE WITH 'EM AT 10 O'CLOCK. THERE SHE GOES.

FOGG AND CANAL STREETS, DRIVER.

YES, MA'AM.

...ND IN A ROOM NOT FAR FROM FOGG AND CANAL STREETS.

I'VE HEARD OF ...LEET FOR YEARS —WIDOW OF THE ...CHEST RACKETEER ...HAT EVER LIVED.

BUT WHY WOULD SHE WANT TO TALK TO US?

LISTEN, IF JOHNNY OF THE "GLASS STEM" IS SENDING HER, THAT'S GOOD ENOUGH FOR ME.

I DON'T GET IT— HUH?

WHILE A WOMAN PRESSES THE BUZZER OF A DOOR ON A DARK AND DREARY STREET, AN "EXPRESSMAN" SORTS HIS PACKAGES.

THE TELEVISION CAMERA

...AM'S GOT THE CAMERA RIGHT ON HER.—GOOD.

Reg. U.S. Pat. Off.:
Copyright, 1949, by The Chicago Tribune.

YOU'RE SURE YOU'LL BE ABLE TO IDENTIFY THOSE MEN IF YOU SEE THEM, FLOSSIE?

ABSOLUTELY, MR. TRACY. I'D **NEVER** FORGET THEM.

THAT'S WHAT I SAID—GENTLEMEN. I WANT TO KILL A COP, AND I WANT YOUR HELP.

THAT "AIN'T THE WAY WE HEERED IT"! IS SLEET REALLY GOING TO PULL A DOUBLE CROSS? AND WHO IS THE "COP"?

1—16—49

69

UNAWARE SHE HAS BEEN FOLLOWED BY SAM CATCHEM IN AN "EXPRESS" TRUCK, SLEET KEEPS HER DATE WITH BIG FROST'S MEN.

YES, I WANT YOU TO DO A JOB FOR ME.

A CERTAIN MAN HAS MADE MY LIFE MISERABLE. HE'S HAUNTED AND PLAGUED ME ALL MY ADULT LIFE. I WANT HIM KILLED!

YOU KNOW DAT'S A NAUGHTY WORD YOU JUST SAID.

IT SURE WAS.

BESIDES, WE'RE BUSINESS MEN. WHAT KIND OF ARGUMENT HAVE YOU GOT? YOU AIN'T SOLD US YET.

JUST A MINUTE, BOYS.

HIS NAME IS CATCHEM— SAM CATCHEM.

WE'VE HEARD OF HIM.

HERE'S 500 IN CASH FOR THE JOB. IS IT A DEAL?

HA! HA! HA! HA!

500, SHE SAYS, GIG! — IMAGINE! AIN'T SHE CUTE?

LISTEN. WE WOULDN'T TOUCH A JOB LIKE THAT FOR LESS'N A GRAND. NOW START TALKING SENSE OR GET OUT OF HERE.

THE 500

LISTEN! YOU WANT SAM CATCHEM BUMPED OFF— YOU WANT US TO DO IT! OUR PRICE IS ONE T'OUSAND FISH.

BUT MY 500—

WE'LL KEEP IT TILL YOU GET ANOTHER 500. GO TO YOUR BANK. BETTER YET, WE'LL GO WITH YOU— TO SEE THAT DIS AIN'T NO TRAP.

THEY'RE COMING OUT, TRACY. HOW'S THE PICTURE COMING IN?

2-WAY WRIST RADIO

TELEGUARD CAMERA

FINE, SAM.

NOW LOOK CLOSELY, FLOSSY. YOU'VE GOT TO IDENTIFY THESE MEN.

70

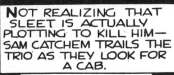

THOSE WERE THE TWO MEN, ALL RIGHT.

I SAW THEIR FACES IN THE TELEVISION VERY PLAINLY! THOSE WERE MY FATHER'S HENCHMEN WHO TRIED TO KILL ME.

"I HAVE A HUNCH YOU'LL HAVE AN OPPORTUNITY TO IDENTIFY THEM FACE TO FACE IN A VERY FEW MINUTES, FLOSSIE." SAYS CHIEF PATTON.

HOLD IT, COPPER, DON'T KILL US! YOU WIN!

FRISK 'EM, SAM. THEY MAY HAVE ANOTHER ROD ON THEM.

NO FIREARMS— BUT, WHU—WHU! LOOK AT THIS ROLL! HUH? GOSH! GET THE AROMA!

ODORA NUMBER FIVE—OR I'M CRAZY! YEAH? PUT IT IN THE BAG AND LET'S GO.

BY THE WAY, WHERE'S SLEET? YEAH—WHAT HAPPENED TO HER?

A SHORT DISTANCE FROM WHERE THE CAPTURE IS TAKING PLACE, A HOUSE IS BEING MOVED.

EVERYTHING'S GONE WRONG! I'M OUT 500 DOLLARS AND THAT FLATFOOT, SAM, IS STILL ALIVE.

BUT I'LL NEVER REST TILL HE GONE. HE'S HAUNTED ME ALL M LIFE—I OUGHT TO—NO—NO—N HERE. I WOULDN'T HAVE A CHANCE.

I CAN'T EXPLAIN IT ENTIRELY, TRACY, BUT I KNOW THE DOUGH IS HERS. SHE'S CLEVER. IT WAS PART OF HER SCHEME. WE GOT OUR MEN, DIDN'T WE? I DON'T GET IT, SAM. I'VE GOT A DIFFERENT SLANT ON THINGS.

LATER

SEVERAL HOURS LATER, AT SLEET'S APARTMENT.

WHAT? WHY, YOU ~*※~! THE NERVE— HOW IN ★~※!! I JUST USED A SPECIAL PASSKEY, SLEET.

Reg. U. S. Pat. Off.: Copyright, 1949, by The Chicago Tribune.

I'VE BEEN WAITING TO RETURN YOUR 500! YOU DID IT, BABY! THIS GUY MAKES THING AWFULLY TOUGH.

1-25-49

DICK TRACY

SCENE: OVERPASS ACROSS THE PARK DRIVE.

BODY IS POISED AT THE RAIL. MOMENT'S HESITATION. THEN, IT PLUNGES DOWNWARD.

THE CREW IS HAVING COFFEE. NO ONE SAW US.

SAM CATCHEM WILL BE COVERED WITH ANOTHER 3 FEET OF SNOW WHEN THE WORKMEN RETURN. THEN, HE'LL BE—

COME! LET'S GET OUT OF HERE.

E DIDN'T KNOW I WAS HIDING IN THE ROOM—-THAT ASH TRAY—THE ETHER--- HA, HA!

LET'S GO!

PARK DIST. 7

WE'RE GOING BACK TO BOSTON. I'LL PACK IMMEDIATELY. WE'LL TAKE THE MORNING PLANE.

MEANWHILE, ON A CORNER NEAR SLEET'S APARTMENT.

HOW DO I KNOW WHOSE IT IS?

ACME CAB

THIS IS MY REGULAR STAND. AT NIGHT AFTER A FARE, I COME BACK HERE—THE GUY WAS STEWED. THE DAMES WERE—

WAIT! I'VE GOT TO GO.

ACME CAB

THERE'S A FIN. I MAY NEED YOU LATER. STAY RIGHT THERE.

ACME CAB

I STILL SAY YOU SHOULD HAVE SHOT HIM.

THEN, WE COULDN'T HAVE WALKED HIM OUT—WE COULDN'T HAVE MOVED HIM. WE'D HAVE HAD A DEAD MAN ON OUR HANDS!

WHAT? THE DOOR'S UNLOCKED!

YOU FORGOT TO SHUT IT. QUICK! INSIDE.

Reg. U.S. Pat. Off.
Copyright, 1949, by The Chicago Tribune.

1-30-49

EVEN NOW, SOME OF THE TRUCKS ARE DUMPING THEIR COLD CARGOES IN THE BAY! IS THIS TO BE THE FATE OF SAM CATCHEM?

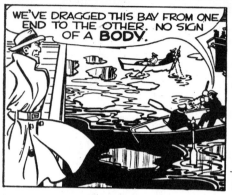

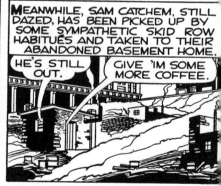

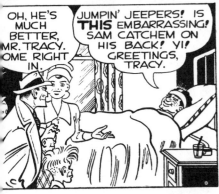  

82

HEY! **OPEN THIS ELEVATOR DOOR!** WHY, THAT --- HEY!

SHE'S GOING UP?

SHE MUST BE GOING TO THE TOP FLOOR. **HEY,** ON FIVE! **STOP THAT WOMAN!**

NOW, TO GO DOWN AGAIN. I CAN'T STAY IN HERE FOREVER!

CHESTER GOULD

THAT'S IT— **PULL THE SWITCH!** WE'LL **CUT** THE JUICE.

BETTER PUT A WATCH ON ALL THE EXITS. SHE'S IN THIS HOSPITAL SOME PLACE.

WHAT A SCANDAL THIS WILL BE! THAT GAL IS A NOTORIOUS CHARACTER.

IT'S **YOUR** FAULT. YOU LEFT HER IN THE ELEVATOR ALONE.

AND IN SAM CATCHEM'S ROOM

LOCKING HERSELF IN A HOSPITAL ELEVATOR, THE WOMAN KNOWN AS SLEET DISAPPEARED BEFORE THE EYES OF STARTLED INTERNES TODAY—

WHAT?

CHESTER GOULD

BELIEVED TO BE SUFFERING FROM POSSIBLE SKULL CONCUSSION, THE BLONDE WAS WHEELED INTO THE ELEVATOR—

NURSE, WHERE'S **MY PANTS?**

SHE'S GOT TO BE **INSIDE** THIS HOSPITAL, MR. TRACY. WATCHES WERE PUT ON THE EXITS IMMEDIATELY.

CURRENT TO THE ELEVATOR WAS FINALLY CUT. UNFORTUNATELY, SHE WENT OUT THE MATERNITY WARD SIDE, AND NOBODY WAS THERE AT THE TIME.

YOWEE! OH—

WHAT'S THAT?

A LITTLE BOY IN 207 IS JUST HAVING HIS BROKEN WRIST BANDAGED

CHESTER GOULD

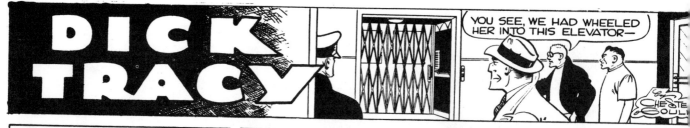

SCENE: COUNTY HOSPITAL— EMERGENCY ENTRANCE.

TO ALL OUTWARD APPEARANCES, SHE WAS STILL UNCONSCIOUS. I STEPPED OUT FOR JUST A SECOND TO ASK CLANCY TO BRING MY TOPCOAT WITH HIM FROM THE AMBULANCE.

NEXT THING I KNEW, THE DOOR SLAMMED SHUT AND THE ELEVATOR WENT UP.

IT'S OBVIOUS SHE WAS FEIGNING UNCONSCIOUSNESS, BUT WHAT ABOUT THE CONDITION OF HER HEAD?

EXAMINATION AT THE JAIL SHOWED SHE HAD AT LEAST ONE SCALP WOUND. SHE WAS BLEEDING

WE DIDN'T SEE HER HERE ON THE SECOND FLOOR, MR. TRACY, BUT SHE MUST HAVE PASSED DOWN THIS HALL.

SAM! WHAT ARE YOU DOING OUT OF BED?

AH—I'M ALL RIGHT!—AND WHEN THEY TOLD ME ABOUT THIS DAME SLEET, I HAD TO GET UP!

I'M GOING TO SEND HER BACK TO BOSTON FOR THE REST OF HER NATURAL LIFE, TRACY, IF IT'S THE LAST THING I DO!

BLOOD SPOTS SHOW SHE APPROACHED THIS TABLE OF TOWELS. ONE WAS USED AND TOSSED ON THE FLOOR.

—AND A NURSE'S COAT IS MISSING.

WHAT'S THIS?

THAT'S THE RAMP FOR WHEEL CHAIR PATIENTS.

AND NOW, THE SCENE CHANGES TO THE ALLEY ENTRANCE OF ONE THE LARGE RESTAURANTS DOWNSTAIRS.

YOU'LL DO. GO DOWNSTAIRS AND WASH UP. YOU'LL FIND A UNIFORM THERE.

DISH WASHER WANTED

Jack's Grille

YOU'LL HANDLE THIS MACHINE AND THIS SINK. NOW, GET BUSY.

YES, SIR.

THEY'RE NOT APT TO LOOK FOR ME IN A RESTAURANT KITCHEN.

MY HEAD STILL HURTS. BUT IT'S ALMOST STOPPED BLEEDING.

Reg. U.S. Pat Off. Copyright, 1949. by The Chicago Tribune.

WELL, I'LL BE— A WHEEL CHAIR!

YOU KNOW, SAM— IT'LL BE NICE TO SEE SPRING ROLL AROUND AGAIN —NO SLEET!

2-20-49

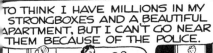

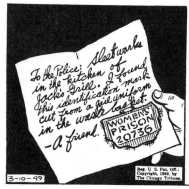

Reg. U. S. Pat. Off.:
Copyright, 1949, by The Chicago Tribune.

H'M—HERE'S A COMPACT MUST HAVE TUMBLED OUT OF HER PURSE WHEN THE WINDOW KNOCKED HER TO THE SIDEWALK.

3-17-49

OH, THANK YOU. YES, IT IS MINE.

Reg. U. S. Pat. Off.: Copyright, 1949, by The Chicago Tribune.

H'M—I SEE SOMETHING ELSE OVER THERE.

PERFUME! H'M? I WONDER IF THAT'S HERS, TOO? AW, I'LL TAKE IT HOME TO MY WIFE.

Odora No 5 Parfum

CHESTER GOULD

THIS IS—ER— A BEAUTIFUL PLACE YOU HAVE HERE.

OH, THANK YOU, MY DEAR.

3-18-49

IT'S QUIET AND HOMEY. I'VE LIVED HERE OVER 40 YEARS.

Reg. U. S. Pat. Off.: Copyright, 1949, by The Chicago Tribune.

YOU'RE MOST AGREEABLE ABOUT THIS ACCIDENT. ANYONE ELSE WOULD HAVE WANTED A SPECIALIST AND A COUPLE OF LAWYERS IMMEDIATELY.

CHESTER GOULD

TELL ME, WHAT KIND OF A HOME IS THIS?— I MEAN WITH ALL THESE STUFFED ANIMALS AND THINGS?

THAT'S A VERY INTERESTING STORY, MY DEAR— AND YOU SHALL HEAR IT.

YOU SEE, MY LATE HUSBAND WAS A COLLECTOR—WORLD FAMOUS.

3-19-49

BUT BEFORE I GO ON, DON'T YOU THINK I SHOULD KNOW SOMETHING ABOUT YOU? WHAT IS YOUR NAME?

Reg. U. S. Pat. Off.: Copyright, 1949, by The Chicago Tribune.

MEANWHILE, THE PAINTERS, WHO HAVE QUIT FOR THE DAY, DROP INTO THE COCKTAIL BAR UP THE STREET.

JUST ONE BEFORE GOING HOME.

Minute Bar

AND AT HEADQUARTERS.

LISTEN! LET'S GO BACK TO THAT COCKTAIL LOUNGE ONCE MORE, TRACY. MAYBE SLEET'S THERE NOW. I TELL YOU IT WAS HER!

OKAY, SAM —ONCE MORE.

CHESTER GOULD

95

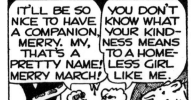

IT'S A WEIRD PLACE, SAM.

I'LL SAY! I DON'T MIND LOCKING HORNS WITH A GANGSTER, BUT THIS STUFF GIVES ME THE CREEPS.

IT SEEMS THERE'S NOBODY HOME BUT THE STUFFED ANIMALS.

EH?

SOMETHING OVER THERE LOOKS HUMAN TO ME.

YOW!

IS—IS SHE ALIVE?

HATCHET FROM CIGAR STORE INDIAN

SHE'S BREATHING. BUT SHE'S OUT COLD! SHE'S GOT A NASTY CUT ON THE HEAD.

THAT MUST BE THE WEAPON LYING ON THE FLOOR.

SLEET IS DESPERATE—BUT WHY WOULD SHE DO A THING LIKE THIS?

THE PLACE IS SURROUNDED—SHE CAN'T GET OUT OF THE BUILDING —OR CAN SHE?

AND ON THE THIRD FLOOR— HATED TO SOCK HER, BUT SHE WOULDN'T GIVE ME HER KEYS! SAID I MUSTN'T GO UPSTAIRS.

THERE'S BOUND TO BE AN OUTLET TO THE ROOF, AND, IF THE ADJOINING BUILDING IS THE SAME HEIGHT, I CAN GO DOWN A FIRE ESCAPE.

MEAL

E-E-E! POOH! JUST MORE SPECIMENS.

THESE STUFFED ANIMALS DON'T FAZE ME ANY MORE! AHA! THIS IS IT! I SEE ANOTHER ROOF.

Reg. U. S. Pat. Off.: Copyright, 1949, by The Chicago Tribune

—BUT I MUST BE SURE THE DOOR IS LOCKED—TO SLOW UP ANY- BODY THAT COMES UP THOSE STAIRS.

3-27-49

DICK TRACY

by CHESTER GOULD

LUCKILY, THE GORILLA, WITH WHICH SLEET FINDS HERSELF PRISONER, IS NOT VICIOUS, BUT HE ROUGH HER CONSIDERABLY AND FRIGHTENS HER TO THE POINT OF HYSTERIA.

YES, DICK TRACY AND SAM CATCHEM HAVE A PLAN AFOOT THAT IS BEGINNING TO WORK.

I'M FREE! I'VE BROKEN AWAY FROM HIM.

THE REASON SLEET HAS BROKEN AWAY IS PLAIN. HAVING FASTENED ANOTHER CHAIN TO THE OUTSIDE END OF THE RING-BOLT, THEY HAVE JERKED THE GORILLA OFF BALANCE AND ARE SNUBBING HIM TOWARD THE WALL.

ONCE MORE, SAM. IF WE GET HIM AGAINST THE WALL, WE CAN CHOKE HIM AND HE'LL **HAVE** TO RELEASE SLEET.

FLAG POLE

HE'S ALREADY **RELEASED** HER! I CAN SEE HER **NOW**!

THAT DOOR UNLOCKS FROM THE INSIDE!

SHE'S OUT! SHE'S RUNNING TOWARD THE REAR OF THE BUILDING.

WE CAN'T DROP THE CHAIN. LET'S SNUB IT TIGHT—TO THE POLE.

SLEET'S DREAM OF ESCAPING ACROSS THE ADJOINING ROOF TOPS GETS A SEVERE JOLT.

IT'S TOO FAR TO JUMP. I—I'LL HAVE TO LEAP TO THE TOP OF THE WATER TANK AND USE THE LADDER.

SHE **JUMPS**! THERE'S A SPLINTERING OF WOOD AS THE TANK'S ROOF SUPPORTS GIVE WAY.

CRASH!

WELL, WHAT DO YOU KNOW, SAM! SHE MUST HAVE STOPPED TO WASH HER FEET! THAT GAUGE SHOWS THERE'S ABOUT 12 FEET OF WATER IN THAT TANK.

GO TO THE SQUAD CAR, SAM. THERE'S A 50-FOOT PIECE OF ROPE IN THE TRUNK.

Reg. U. S. Pat. Off.:
Copyright, 1949, by The Chicago Tribune.

H'M? IT'S APRIL 3RD. SPRING IS HERE AT LAST. — AND SPRING MEANS THE LAST OF SLEET.

4-3-49

YES, SLEET, THOSE WATER TANK ROOFS USUALLY DEVELOP A LITTLE DAMP ROT. THEY'RE NOT TO BE TRUSTED.

HERE'S THE ROPE, TRACY. *YIPEE! LASSOO* HER? SHOULD I

I'M AN OLD COW-HAND—

EASY, NOW, SAM. THIS CALLS FOR DEXTERITY AND SKILL—

—I THEENK.

SLEET, IT LOOKS LIKE A NICE, WARM SUMMER AHEAD. BUT YOU WON'T BE HOT. YOU'LL BE IN THE COOLER.

NOW, IF YOU'LL SAY GOODBYE TO MRS. INDIA AND THANK HER FOR HER HOSPITALITY—WE'LL BE ON OUR WAY.

THE DEPARTMENT WILL SEND A MAN UP TO MEND THE HOLE IN THE BRICK MASONRY AND RESET THE GORILLA'S CHAIN.

EVEN THE DARK DUNGEONS OF YOUR DIRTY POLICE BUILDING WILL BE BETTER THAN THIS HORROR CHAMBER. UGH! LET'S GO.

EASY, BABY, EASY.

APRIL IN PARIS

APRIL *IN* SOLITARY UM DE DE DA DA DA DA!

I'VE JUST CHECKED THE TIMETABLE OF TRAINS GOING EAST. SLEET WILL LEAVE HERE AT 12:30 P.M.

THE BOYS FROM BOSTON WILL BE IN TO PICK YOU UP ABOUT ELEVEN O'CLOCK. HAVE A NICE TRIP, BABY!

I KINDA HATE TO SEE THAT DAME GO, TRACY. SHE AT LEAST FURNISHED A LITTLE EXCITEMENT.

YES, SAM, IT'S APT TO BE A LITTLE DULL AROUND HERE, NOW.

AND NOT TOO FAR AWAY.

OWOOO OWOOo WOOO

The Aesthetics of Dick Tracy

by Richard Marschall

Even a casual reader of Dick Tracy finds his memory's dam bursting with recollections...and images.

In the early years, the characters who were overcome by realizations or separations, their eyes bulging maniacally...the washed-down street scenes, the invariably impersonal cityscapes, the darkness overhead and round the corner...the fascination, like Hitchcock's, with innocent citizens drawn into menacing webs...and Tracy's grim profile and the chase.

In the later years we had the bizarre villains and ghastly deeds...crimefighting technologies...a gallery of grotesque faces and singular names...overt violence...and Tracy's grim profile and the chase.

In the final years of Chester Gould's involvement there were some new cops...Tracy's crewcut and moustache...trips to the moon...law-and-order sermons...and Tracy's grim profile and the chase.

Dick Tracy began as much as an editorial as it did an entertainment feature. It was to transcend both functions. With single-minded, almost fierce, resolve, Chester Gould set the following thematic course at the beginning: Crime is ugly, and organized crime is pernicious. No citizen is safe, and too often the decent, hard-working Joe minding his own business is drawn into horrific circumstances; all people suffer from crime, indirectly at least. That the criminal has put himself outside the community's legal pale will—should?—result in that criminal being pursued, overtaken, and punished, sometimes on the ground he has chosen. Police are sworn to uphold the law but in a larger sense they must preside over True Justice being served. They know True Justice in the larger sense, and so does the criminal in the end, whatever that end may be. The average citizen recognized it, too. And so do average newspaper readers.

Gould had established a marvelous formula. Dick Tracy became a morality play, a panorama of good guys and bad guys, an opportunity to concoct clever mysteries and squeeze every ounce from their solutions. Morality plays are not supposed to be subtle. Everything in Gould's world was black and white. An appropriate manifestation of the strip's essence is that Dick Tracy Sunday pages are among the few that look to be without color.

Of comic strips, more than any other art form, purportedly serious critics will often seek out the worst of the form—an ill-conceived creation, poorly drawn attempts—instead of judging the better manifestations.

Less perceptive critics have depicted Chester Gould as a purveyor of violence and primitivistic images. But Dick Tracy is a reflection of human emotions, a moralistic evocation of the system where fatalistic retribution reigns; and a glorious graphic masterpiece.

Gould always knew exactly what he was doing. The entire run of Dick Tracy is a parade of changing, brooding, threatening, underlying moods. Occasionally violence breaks the tension. When it does it's as severe and ugly as in real life. But these spurts of physical action are only slight pressure valves; the tension, the implied and imminent violence, yet lurks—in people, in events, in all the environment.

The primary vehicle for this mood-setting is characterization, of which Chester Gould is the acknowledged master in his field. In the thirties, the villains were cruelly ruthless, in the forties eccentric, but they form only part of the recipe. The settings and background play a large role. Gould masterfully used black areas and shadows to convey mood, impersonality and loneliness.

Gould used soliloquies; the hunter and hunted—the lone hero cop and the desperate killer, not necessarily in that order—to boldly present characters to the reader, stripped of encumbrances.

When violence is shown, often enough it's used with a legitimate purpose. Not

JUST WAIT AND WATCH. GOT YOUR MAGNUM READY, SAM?

AND HOW!

10-8-61

CHESTER GOULD

only does good triumph, but Gould's villains are bad—and not bad because they have funny names and faces. No, his villains kidnap children and shoot innocent citizens. And they receive ultimate justice by their code or ours. Of the great unrecognized triumphs of Gould's work, the most deserved of study is that, as a comic strip artist, his violence was understated. With all the punches, all the explosions, all the bullets finding their mark, the artist very seldom used the tired crutches of onomatopoeia. You will very seldom see bangs or bams or ka-blams in Dick Tracy; the violence, as are all the elements, is muted and kept from trivialization.

Storytelling elements are just as important as visual elements in Dick Tracy and reveal Gould's mastery as completely as the best movie director's or author's. His pacing could be frenetic or excruciatingly slow—and frequently was both simultaneously. The Sunday page for March 21, 1954, which accompanies this essay, cuts between Dewdrop's murder of her father to the police station grilling of Mrs. Green on

another perversity, child abandonment. The contrasts of the murder act versus stoicism, the dark bedroom versus the glaring police lights, the very audacity of including both plot elements at no expense to either show Gould at his best. That all factors combine to arrest the eye and the interest of the reader gives us one of the gestalt delights that is a fringe benefit of the comic strip.

Likewise, the December 16, 1957, daily with Tracy and his adopted son Junior in front of the fireplace in a very personal exchange uses visuals to set mood, draw the interest and mirror the characters' emotions. Knowing when to stop, Gould's employment of shadows is effective and his contrasts striking, but every shot is middle-ground; varying the camera angles would have been a visual temptation, but would have detracted from the all-important dialogue of this particular interlude.

Throughout the strip Gould would use silent panels, sometimes Sunday pages totally without dialogue, stark backgrounds including blinding white; he would drop

Gould has kept Tracy in the fashion of the day. Here on September 30, 1956, Tracy receives a crew haircut. Later, in the early 1970's, he would wear his hair fashionably longer. At one point, Tracy also sported a moustache, which he wore for several years. But as with anything in Dick Tracy, even a haircut can lead to bigger things: a shot through the window, a kid with a body in front of her, and a smoking gun.

details, and elevate incidental elements. In a sense Tracy was Tracy as much for what it did not show.

Chester Gould, like his closest peer and technical cousin Harold Gray ("Little Orphan Annie"), was never a realist, even an unfulfilled one. These men were both Expressionists, and wildly successful in their approach. Their Expressionistic techniques pervaded every element of their creations—the art, the storytelling, the dialogue, the compositions, the pacing—and so created quintessential examples of what the comic strip can be as an independent art form.

A few technical details should reveal something of Gould's strictures and his triumph over them. It was a tradition in his syndicate to have the same storyline in daily strips and Sunday pages, but to make them independent of each other. The strip had to be fashioned so as to be intelligible to Sunday-only or six-days-a-week-only readers, even though very few of those creatures probably ever existed. So it fell to artists to merely recap the week's action in the Sunday page. Gould seized on it as a superb vehicle for depicting action and maturing his characterizations. Also, the weird effects in the dailies—those large, open spaces and solid blacks along panel bottoms—were the result of another imposition. The syndicate decreed that the bottom portion of dailies should be expendable to allow certain newspaper clients to shave the strips and fit more on a page. An absurd strait-jacket, or waste, to some, but Gould turned it around and

The master at expressing mood and foreboding, Chester Gould's black and white stylized swirling water complements the coming frenzy of the sharks as Ivy's horrific departure from this earth is assured by a nosebleed.

The advancement of two separate plot developments, murder and child
abandonment, fill the Sunday page for March 21, 1954, with the contrast
between an act of murder as Dewdrop smothers her own father and the
stoicism of Mrs. Green as she is grilled at the police station. The darkness
of the sickroom equals the darkness of the crime of patricide.

The static pattern of Gould's presentation of Junior and Tracy sitting in
front of a fire discussing life remind one of today's "Doonesbury" artwork
by Gary Trudeau, except that Trudeau doesn't use the strong shadows that
Gould used. The text is what is important in this daily, and the mood of
warmth and closeness. The pattern of the couch's placement forward and
back in the alternating panels creates a marvelous sigzag for the reader's
eye to follow.

In Chester Gould's later work, simplification of line and design are key elements. Master of the cliff-hanger, Gould knew the spirit of Christmas and a life-and-death drama were attention grabbers. To add a third element to an attention-getting Sunday page, Gould makes the most of Lizz's curvy figure, dressing her in a mini-skirt and drawing her bust in profile. Drama, God and sex are combined in a skillful manner.

achieved positive design elements.

Rarely did Gould subordinate these strong aesthetic tendencies. Rarely has there been such a sustained—literally lifetime—high level of quality in the popular arts or any art form.

Chester Gould set his sights high with Dick Tracy—aiming for popular acceptance, rich characterization, lively action, visual appeal (black and white would always be his most effective colors), a mixture of humor, tension, violence, pain and joy. That Gould was doing something right could never have been in doubt, as dominance of readership in polls and widespread merchandising attest. It is rewarding that critical acclaim for Dick Tracy by Chester Gould has secured for Gould an important place in 20th-century popular culture.

This single panel reproduced in the size of the original drawing shows the maturing of the abstract design elements in Gould's work as he strove to grab the viewer's attention and tell a story. The head is eliminated to emphasize the gun in the woman's back. Her bust and sexy turn of leg are shown to catch the male reader's eye.

25th Anniversary

Dick Tracy Anniversary For Release On or After Sunday, October 14, 1956, By Charles Collins

CHICAGO, OCT. 13 (CTPS).—Dick Tracy, the most modern and famous of fictitious detectives, was born twenty-five years ago this month in two newspapers, the New York *News* and the Detroit *Mirror*. His appearance in the Chicago *Tribune*, which became his headquarters, was delayed until January 24, 1932. He now flourishes in more than 450 newspapers which reach between 60 and 70 million readers and are circulated on three continents.

Tracy's creator, Chester Gould, has almost ignored his birthday. He is always too busy at his drawing board to be aware of such impressive occasions. But he has only to lift his eyes off his work to see proof that 25 years have passed since Tracy's natal day. Over his desk is a framed page from the New York *News* on which the first episode in Tracy's career is depicted.

Gould has been told that a suitable memorial would be a silver-plated automobile, custom-built with gadgets for housekeeping to simulate the machine in which his latest and most fantastic villain, Flattop Jr., baffled pursuers for months. But he thinks that Tracy would not approve of such a symbol for the glorification of the misdeeds of juvenile delinquents. His only birthday gift to Dick was a crew haircut.

When Tracy sprang full-grown from the Gould imagination he was an amateur detective, quite unlike Sherlock Holmes, especially in the scholarship of criminology. Thereby hangs a tale. When Captain Joseph Medill Patterson, late publisher of the New York *News*, had glanced at the first drawings of Tracy from the pen of a novice cartoonist, he told their creator:

"Start him off as an ordinary young fellow who has dedicated himself to the pursuit of thugs who have murdered the father of the girl he loves. After he succeeds in bringing them to justice, you might turn him into a professional police officer."

So during the first few weeks of his life, Dick Tracy was merely a police "buff"—a hard-hitting amateur who dealt with crim-

inals with fists, blackjack, or gun. His prowess won an unsought appointment as a city detective.

In that period, Tracy was drawn as a more comic figure than the character of his international fame who rarely smiles and then only on one side of his face. His first hat, for example, had an undented stovepipe crown and a stiff brim turned down all around. It suggested a comic characterization of a Korean mandarin. Moreover, the figure was often drawn full length and seemed gawky.

Today, Tracy is usually seen in close-up portraiture—full face or head and shoulders. He immediately impresses his observers as a character commanding deep respect, an indomitable take-charge fellow in every emergency.

* * *

His career started with a proposal of marriage, which was interrupted by assassins' guns when the girl was about to say "yes." But 18 years elapsed before Dick was able to carry his bride over the threshold of their home, and during the long wait neither had aged perceptibly.

That long period of celibacy is to be accounted for by the first law of crime stories: Great detectives should always be bachelors. This precept, however, has been faithfully observed only by Sherlock Holmes, who had a narrow escape from a blackmailing charmer named Irene Adler, and by Hercule Poirot, who was too old for matrimony and too cynical to try his luck anyway.

Although Tracy married and became a father, Chester Gould has revealed little about his hero's family life. None of the drawings have depicted him as a husband returning to his home after a hard day's work, latchkey in hand and grocery parcels under his arm. Nobody knows where he sleeps. It is possible that, according to the motto of the Pinkertons, he never sleeps.

The city that breeds the criminal freaks and monsters who provide Tracy with mys-

teries to solve could be Chicago, of course, since Chester Gould works here and is always in close touch with the technical experts of the police laboratories. But the scenes in these panels of drawings, day after day, might be placed in any large American City. Gould always avoids localization of detail, even in street names and bits of architecture.

The deserted theater in which Flattop Jr. came to his theoretical end a few weeks ago could easily be in Chicago, which has many similar edifices awaiting demolition. But such relics of the era of entertainment that flourished before movies, radio, and television can be found all over the United States.

Gould came to Chicago in 1921, after three years at Oklahoma A&M College in Stillwater, not far from his birthplace (November 20, 1900), Pawnee, Oklahoma, a county seat. At college he had been active on student publications as a cartoonist,

and he hoped that he could find employment in some advertising agency. But he had no formal training in drawing, and when his samples failed to interest personnel managers he became a student again at Chicago art schools and Northwestern University, from which he was graduated in 1924. Then he got a small-salaried job with the Hearst newspapers as a minor cartoonist.

During this period he showered newspapers and syndicates with examples of his work. They were invariably returned without favorable comment. Finally, he invented Tracy, whom he nicknamed "Plain Clothes." His colleagues told him there was no hope of his selling such bloodthirsty episodes as a comic strip. But when the publisher of the New York *News* found "Plain Clothes Tracy" in his mailbag, he arranged to interview Tracy's unknown inventor in Chicago. With a few suggestions, Captain Patterson put the young artist on

the right track toward fame and fortune.

In 1936, after Gould's income from the syndication of the Dick Tracy story became handsome, he established his family home on a 130-acre farm near Woodstock, Illinois. This county seat, about 50 miles northwest of Chicago in the Fox River valley, has none of the characteristics of a suburban community. It is mellow with the traditions of country life in a landscape of notable charm. Its population, about 6,000, descends from the pioneers of the region. Its business center is formed around a public square, well shaded on warm summer days.

One of the buildings on the square at Woodstock contains the town offices and jail, and also an old theater which provided dramatic stars on tour between the Civil and the Spanish-American Wars with a one-night stand. Twenty-two years ago, a gifted lad named Orson Welles, educated at the Todd School for Boys on the edge of town, organized and staged an ambitious summer drama festival in that ancient playhouse.

One night when the young genius Welles was co-starring with two actors from the Gate Theatre of Dublin in a revival of *Trilby*, a rival drama was in progress before the town justice downstairs. To the utter delight of attending sophisticates from Chicago, a shotgun wedding was performed there.

If Chester Gould had been a Woodstock citizen then, the incident might have suggested a passage in the Dick Tracy saga.

In a publicity photo taken in 1963, Chester Gould reads his Dick Tracy Sunday page as published in his "hometown" newspaper, the ChicagoTribune. Assistant Jack Ryan is behind him.

A Double Reuben Man: Chester Gould and the National Cartoonists Society

Chester Gould was a great supporter of the National Cartoonists Society (NCS) and truly enjoyed the fellowship of the organization.

The Reuben award for "Outstanding Cartoonist of the Year" is often compared with the Oscar for the movie industry. The Reuben is the highest award a cartoonist can receive from his peers. Selection is made by the secret ballot of the members of the NCS. Traditionally the award is presented at the annual NCS banquet held most years in New York City during the Newspaper Publishers' convention.

Unlike the heroic looking Oscar, the Reuben is a jumble of Nibelungs or Kilroys that capture the irreverent spirit of cartooning. The bronze statuette was designed by Rube Goldberg and sculpted by Bill Crawford.

"The Reuben is pure fantasy," wrote its designer, Rube Goldberg, "including the bottle of india ink that Bill Crawford placed on the posterior of the top man to give the design a little more symmetry. If the Reuben has an underlying significance in its present form, I will say that I created it to keep it from looking like a golf trophy, an Oscar, or a statuette presented to Miss Kitchen Utensils of 1953. My only hope is that each recipient will look upon it as a symbol of the admiration and love of his fellow cartoonists."

Few cartoonists ever win the Reuben. Chester Gould is in that elite circle that has won the Reuben twice, first in 1959 and

Rube Goldberg presents Chester Gould with the National Cartoonists Society's "Reuben" award for Cartoonist of the Year 1959. Gould won the award a second time in 1977. Goldberg designed the award, a precarious tower of four naked imps crowned with an ink bottle, so it wouldn't look like a bowling trophy.

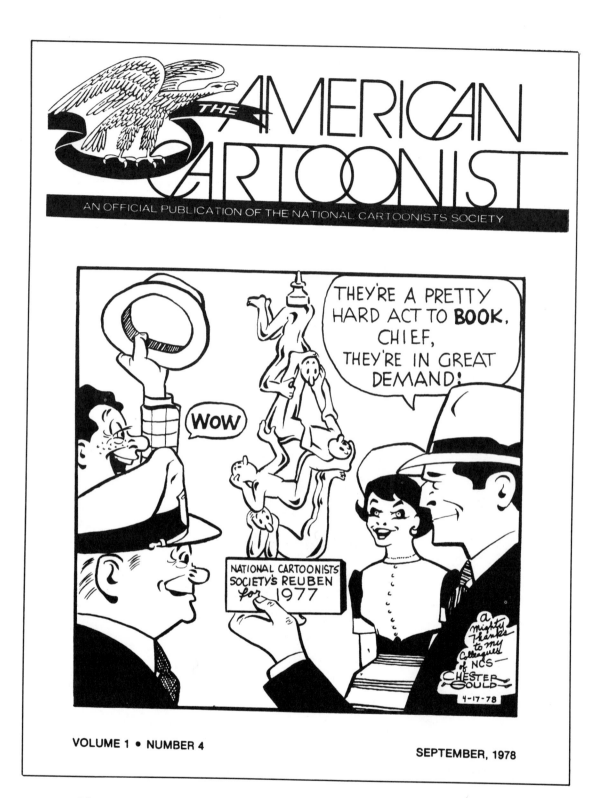

After winning the Reuben award for 1977, which was awarded at the
annual NCS dinner in April 1978, Gould drew this special cover
illustration for the NCS's *The American Cartoonist*.

then in 1977. Others include Milton Caniff of "Terry and the Pirates" and "Steve Canyon" fame, Charles "Peanuts" Schultz, Dik Browne of "Hagar the Horrible" and "Hi & Lois," and Pulitzer-winning editorial cartoonist and the father of "Shoe," a humor strip, Jeff MacNelly.

Over the years the program for the annual Reuben award's dinner has developed into an elaborate booklet filled with special drawings by many internationally famed cartoonists. These special drawings don't come cheap. The dinner is a fund-raiser for the Society's Milt Gross Fund, which helps cartoonists in hard times. Each participating cartoonist—and all members have the opportunity—pays a goodly donation for the privilege of having his or her artwork published in the program.

The NCS was founded in 1946 by five working cartoonists: Rube Goldberg, Russell Paterson, Gus Edson, Clarence Russell and Otto Soglow. Given the importance of cartooning in American popular culture, it is amazing that no national organization for cartoonists was started earlier.

NCS meetings are always friendly and at times raucous. Cartoonists love to flaunt their spirit of rebellion and this spirit accompanies them to meetings. Guests are often humorously jibed by the toastmaster. And members receiving honors are sometimes cheerfully lambasted at the same time they are cheered.

Rube Goldberg was one of the pillars of the NCS and at times the organization functions as one of his famous Rube Goldberg Inventions, "a humorously complicated device of many diverse and illogical parts working together to achieve a logical if sometimes trivial goal."

While the organization exists for fellowship, the NCS has over the years supported many charitable and patriotic causes. Especially well-known is its art program in support of U.S. Savings Bonds.

This section is illustrated with a portfolio of some of Gould's special drawings for NCS Reuben Awards programs.

AS THE CARTOONIST, CONTINUOUSLY WRITING AND DRAWING HIS ORIGINAL COMIC STRIP CREATION — 6 DAILY STRIPS AND A SUNDAY PAGE — 365 DAYS A YEAR FOR THE MOST NUMBER OF YEARS, FROM OCT. 4, 1931 TO DECEMBER 25, 1977 — FORTY SIX YEARS, TWO MONTHS AND 21 DAYS — GOULD SET A RECORD WITH DICK TRACY.

ALSO, BEING ON THE FRONT PAGE OF A NEW YORK CITY METROPOLITAN NEWSPAPER COMIC SECTION — NAMELY THE NEW YORK NEWS — BEGINNING IN 1932, 45 YEARS — PLUS! — AN ALL-TIME RECORD.

CHESTER GOULD

Celebrated Cases

The single constant theme that ran throughout all the years of the Dick Tracy strip was that crime doesn't pay. Tracy had many celebrated cases. Of which most ended with the demise of the villain. When it came to malicious men and vicious vixens, Dick Tracy was a harsh nemesis.

Gould came up with a small filler feature titled "Dick Tracy Says" in the early 1950s. It featured one-column-wide artwork and a quote from Dick Tracy. Perhaps the most appropriate, given the fate of so many of Tracy's opponents, is "They said he was a smart crook, but who ever heard of a bullet being afraid of brains."

World War II is credited by Gould with making Flattop and The Brow two of his most famous villains. The Brow in Gould's opinion also met the most grizzly end, skewered on a flagpole.

"The meanest character that Tracy's ever met is without a doubt Mrs. Pruneface," says Gould. "She's the one who tried to dispose of Tracy by the fiendish scheme of resting an icebox on two 100-pound cakes of ice. As they melted the weight of the refrigerator would drive a steel spike through Tracy's heart. Tracy escaped, narrowly, when he discovered that by bumping the floor, he could move the melting ice just enough that the spike barely misses him."

This section highlights a few of Tracy's many memorable cases.

Spaldoni (1934)

When George Spaldoni, a crooked lawyer, discovers that author Jean Penfield's manuscript will expose his lucrative underworld connections, he has her killed. The fingerprints of Tess Trueheart, Tracy's sweetheart, are planted on the murder weapon. After some gruelling detective work, Dick Tracy, aided by his adopted son Junior, corners Spaldoni and his gang in an abandoned steel mill. Spaldoni makes a fatal mistake in trying to shoot it out with Dick Tracy. Dying, the crooked lawyer clears Tess just before he expires.

Nuremoh (Homerun spelled backwards) (1939)

Although engaged to Dick Tracy in 1931, Tess Trueheart's relationship with Tracy had its ups and downs. He obviously wasn't the easiest fellow to catch and the marriage was delayed until December 25, 1949.

No doubt frustrated by Tracy's devotion to his work and the numerous smokescreens put up to postpone a trip to the altar, Tess meets and marries Nuremoh, a former professional baseball player in 1939.

Nuremoh proves to be not as mentally stable as Tess at first thinks. Infuriated when his rich aunt changes her will in favor of another nephew, Nuremoh kills the woman on his own wedding day. Tess is mortified, almost literally, when she finds out about the deed and Nuremoh tries to kill her. Dick Tracy is at hand to save her, but it is Nuremoh's former mistress who throws herself into the path of the bullet meant for Tess.

His mind completely gone, Nuremoh gathers his former lover up in his arms and, clutching her body, leaps to his death off a cliff. Chester Gould's tale of a wedding gone sour from 1939 certainly matches anything to be seen on the evening television soaps such as "Dallas" or "Dynasty."

B-B Eyes (1942)

Named for his beady-eyed stare, this crook trafficked in bootleg tires. Revenge for the death of his brother at Tracy's hands was his motive for trying to kill the detective. On separate occasions B-B Eyes had Tracy and his sidekick, Pat Patton, sealed in warm paraffin, and then tried to steam Tracy to death. However, Tracy cornered the gang and arrested B-B Eyes. In an attempt to escape, the scoundrel leaped from the lower level of a bridge onto a garbage scow passing underneath. Lying

in the slime, muck and rubbish on the scow, B-B Eyes ironically met his death immobilized by a discarded tire and unceremoniously dumped into the ocean.

Pruneface (1942)

World War II is the background for one of Gould's more bizarre villains. A spy and saboteur, Pruneface by chance rented a room from Mrs. Trueheart, Tracy's mother-in-law to be. He had a typewriter that was really a disguised radio, and an umbrella that concealed the aerial.

Pruneface's goal was to destroy a bombsight factory nearby. His method involved sending a nitro-loaded pulley machine down an inclined train track. However, he's foiled by an alert Tess and her mother. The chase begins with Tracy in hot pursuit.

A broken leg slows down Pruneface, and his fellow spy, Number Twenty, kidnaps a

doctor and hijacks an ambulance to help his shrivel-faced accomplice. However, Tracy tracks them to their hideout and outfoxes them. Pruneface is captured, battered but alive. Tracy doesn't want to kill a spy who can reveal information on sabotage in America. Still Pruneface's future was simple according to Tracy: "Hospital, county jail, and electric chair."

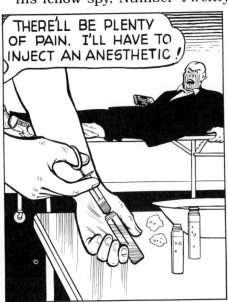

88 Keyes (1943)

Gould's attention turned to high society with this tale of greed and murder. Famed society orchestra leader 88 Keyes arranges for the murder of millionaire A.B. Helmut. Keyes then takes off with Helmut's widow and $200,000 in insurance money. Love is fleeting and he quickly tires and disposes of her. Although temporarily able to outwit Tracy in a railroad station, 88 Keyes expires via the hot lead route in a railroad shack while waiting to hop a freight.

Flattop (1944)

A cold-blooded contract killer named by Gould for the World War II aircraft carriers that had captured the public's imagination, Flattop is hired by black marketeers to kidnap and kill Dick Tracy. However, he double-crosses his customers and tries to up the ante. Held captive by Flattop amid the black marketeers, Tracy breaks loose and grabs a tommy gun. As bullets fly, Tracy yells, "Come on, you mugs, start eating a little of this." Only Flattop escapes and the pursuit is on. During his flight he encounters a pill-popping, has-been actor, Vitamin Flintheart, whom he mugs and steals makeup from. Thus disguised Flattop escapes, but Tracy's pursuit hounds him.

Flattop seeks to hide in a replica of one of

Christopher Columbus's ships anchored in the city's lagoon. Tracy discovers him. In desperation a wounded Flattop tries to swim through the pilings holding the ship in place. He accidently becomes wedged in the pilings and drowns.

The Brow (1944)

A Nazi spy who uses the Summer sisters, a pair of stage-struck pickpockets, as couriers. Tracy first busts the sisters and after their escape he accidently discovers a much more worthy quarry, The Brow. The spy is dedicated to his fiendish task; he is totally amoral, murderous, and a very dangerous opponent. When the sisters are put into protective custody as key witnesses against The Brow, the Nazi kills them.

However, his main task now is survival and escape from Dick Tracy. His bloody trail finally leads him to the isolated shack of Gravel Gertie, who makes her debut in the strip.

The Brow's injuries have temporarily blinded him. He doesn't realize the tender nursing, the soft voice and the silky long hair all belong to a woman whose face would sink a thousand ships. Helen of Troy she ain't. When The Brow finally sees the love-starved Gertie, he has to bite her to get her to let go of him. In the struggle an oil lamp is knocked over and Gertie's home destroyed. She has previously lied to Tracy to protect her newfound love. The Brow is captured when Tracy, checking a field at night near the former Gravel Gertie homestead, hears the spy moan when he hits an electric control cattle fence. Tracy, in a patriotic fervor, discards his weapon and takes The Brow apart with his bare fists. "I'm going to put another wrinkle in that Brow," shouts Tracy as he gives the spy what for.

However, back at headquarters the still love-struck Gertie helps The Brow try one more escape. Tracy foils it by hurling an ink well at The Brow's head that causes the Nazi to reel out a window and fall ironically to his death, skewered by a flagpole in the neighborhood honor roll and service memorial square.

Breathless Mahoney (1946)

The sexy but mean-spirited stepdaughter of the ill-fated extortionist Shakey, she was responsible for her own mother's death in order not to have to share Shakey's ill-gotten gains. Shakey had died in 1945 when he had hidden from Dick Tracy in a coffin of ice under an old filled-in pier. He simply froze to death.

Breathless commits two murders in her escape from a pursuing Tracy. She also meets and is protected from the police by B.O. Plenty, an eccentric bachelor recluse. Sick from hiding in damp soil in a plowed field, Breathless is apprehended by Tracy at B.O.'s farm. However, she still has a bag of tricks.

Doctoring some coffee with rat poison, Breathless puts Tracy out of commission. She then flees with B.O. Plenty and the Shakey fortune, to which B.O. has become attached and is not inclined to share. He too is almost done in by the rat poison. When they meet again he has revenge and money on his mind.

As a subplot, B.O. Plenty and Gravel Gertie meet and fall in love. However, their wedding takes a dramatic turn when B.O. is arrested. Breathless, in custody after B.O. tried to kill her and left her for dead, does die in the prison hospital. She was the only state witness against B.O. Plenty and the case is dropped. Just before her death Breathless scrawls a note, "Give him another chance. I forgive him." It is a new beginning for B.O. Plenty, who becomes a semi-reformed character still plenty rough around the edges.

Mumbles (1947)

The leader of a quartet of organized society robberies, Mumbles is tracked down by Tracy after he blackmails singer Kis Andtel and threatens to scar her face with acid. In the final chase Mumbles escapes by boat. Tracy pursues him in a helicopter. Mumbles takes to a small raft, but his paddle breaks. Trying to attract the attention of a passing boat, Mumbles accidently jabs the inflatable raft with the jagged end of the broken paddle. Swimming isn't Mumbles' strong suite. He sinks and never surfaces.

Mr. Bribery and Ugly Christine (1965)

This charming and deadly brother-sister team surfaced when Ugly Christine took part in an attempted kidnapping of Honeymoon, offspring of Junior Tracy and the celestial Moon Maid. Her brother, Mr. Bribery, was a wheeler-dealer who predated today's Wall Street crooks. He had lots of money, much of it ill-gained, and few scruples. His pet was a shifty-eyed cigar smoking cat. All his aids, including Ugly Christine, bore a mark of allegiance to him in the form of the letter "B" branded into their skin.

With his sister's help, Mr. Bribery was illegally gaining an interest in a takeover bid for Diet Smith Industries, developer of the two-way wrist radio and TV and many other innovations used by Dick Tracy. Things quickly escalated to murder as the severity of the pair's crimes increased.

Ultimately Dick Tracy cracked the case and Ugly Christine met an ugly end, plunging into a smoking smokestack atop a building while trying to avoid arrest. Mr. Bribery's end was equally final.

Scorpio (1969)

This corpulent astrology freak murdered a syndicated horoscope columnist when said columnist made a "mistake" with Scorpio's chart. A bank robber who put his faith in the stars, Scorpio replaced his deceased former adviser with a more reliable, albeit kidnapped, astrologer.

Dick Tracy and Lizz begin with a pair of zodiac cufflinks as their only clue. The trail leads to England where Tracy is assisted by Scotland Yard. Ultimately Scorpio's accomplice Taurus makes the fatal mistake of trying to shoot it out with Tracy and is killed. Scorpio is captured and tried with what Tracy calls "an airtight murder case" against him.

Johnny Scorn and The Pouch (1971)

Johnny Scorn had two addictions, popcorn and dealing in stolen silver and jewels. His courier is former circus fatman, The Pouch. Rapid weight loss had left The Pouch covered with pockets of flesh all over his body. However, his multi-fold neck was equipped with a snap closure and could

hide everything from jewels to a revolver. His former partner, jewel thief and disguise artist, Chameleon, died after a wild snowmobile chase and shootout with Tracy. However, a talent such as The Pouch's didn't wait long for another employer.

Molene, the niece of ex-con The Mole (he first appeared in 1941) guides The Pouch into the service of Johnny Scorn. Molene, who lives a subterranean life, has a serious crush on Johnny Scorn. He, however, scorns her in favor of a very hot and dangerous lady, El Tigress, a svelte revolutionary with a passion for jewelry as well as politics. Jealousy leads Molene to dynamite herself and her rival to the hereafter. Johnny Scorn, however, escapes death at the hands of Molene. Rather, he is killed by an enraged Pouch who discovered counterfeit instead of real money was used to pay for his courier services. Johnny Scorn goes to the big popcorn popper in the sky after Pouch sabotages his popper with some dynamite.

So of this whole motley crew, The Pouch ultimately must face capture by Dick Tracy.

Angeltop (1978 and 1982)

Angelica "Angeltop" Jones, daughter of contract killer Flattop who died trying to escape Dick Tracy in 1944, came to the city to hype her book *Sins of the Father: My Life as Flattop's Daughter*. However, her real purpose was to settle some scores. Not only had her father died being pursued by Tracy, but her brother, Flattop, Jr., at the tender age of 18 had been shot and killed by policewoman Lizz after he'd been on a criminal tear.

Aided by The Brow's son, Angeltop sets her planned revenge in motion. Vitamin Flintheart is shot and only by chance not killed. Tracy falls into the hands of Angeltop who has him transported to the same location at which her father died, the replica of Columbus's ship in the city lagoon.

Bound, gagged and trussed up, Tracy gets an icy bath as Angeltop kicks him into the water and has him wedged in the same set of pilings her father died in. Only the

arrival of Lizz, Sam Catchem, and Groovy Grove from Tracy's unit saves the day. In the shootout that follows, a kerosene lamp turns the ship into an inferno. Angeltop is presumed dead.

But, disfigured by the fire and her mane of hair scorched off her head, Angeltop is far from dead. However, she doesn't resurface for four years.

Then with a face restored by Dr. Carver, the underworld plastic surgeon, she renews her quest for revenge. Carver she rewards for a job well done by killing him.

By this time Angeltop's mind has completely snapped. She is still assisted by The Brow's son, who is in love with her, but he has turned out to be a real wimp. His father would be ashamed of him.

Her plan this time is to blow up the entire Tracy family and their friends with a bomb placed in the church's basement during the wedding of Junior Tracy and Sparkle Plenty. She also kidnaps Lizz the policewoman whom she wants to kill separately. Ultimately her wimpish boyfriend sells Angeltop down the river and releases Lizz, who foils this bloody revenge plan.

Angeltop had entered the realm of the criminally insane. She was institutionalized.

Not nearly as well known as his famous "Crimestoppers" series, "Dick Tracy Says" was created by Gould in the early 1950's. In the fundamental crime-does-not-pay world of Dick Tracy, these homespun one-liners have validity. In the real world they make one laugh at their corniness, but they entertain, which Gould always stated was his purpose.

GENIUS ? **CRIMINAL ?**

Chester Gould's Last Story

AT THE GOVERNOR'S REQUEST, AUTHORITIES GRANT DADE PLENTY EIGHT HOURS' LEAVE TO SUPERVISE THE FITTING OF HIS EVENING DRESS DESIGN FOR THE GOVERNOR'S WIFE.

The STATE CAPITOL

GOVERNOR'S MANSION

REMEMBER, HANDCUFFS ARE OFF NOW, SO WATCH YOUR STEP.

SO YOU'RE THE YOUNG DESIGNER!

THIS IS MY DRESSMAKER, MINDY.

SHALL WE GET STARTED, MADAM?

WE MUST GET THE PRECISE DRAPE BEFORE CUTTING A PATTERN.

ONE HOUR LATER

AND NOW, MADAM, YOU AND THE DESIGNER IN ONE FOR THE PRESS.

CHESTER GOULD

8-7-77 WHAT WILL ALL THIS LEAD TO?

© 1977 by The Chicago Tribune
All Rights Reserved

CRIMESTOPPERS TEXTBOOK

SOMEONE SIPHONED THE GAS OUT OF YOUR TANK?

MOTORISTS: FOR ECONOMY'S SAKE, LOCK CAR IN GARAGE AT NIGHT, OR BUY A GASOLINE TANK LOCK.

Dick Tracy

Panel 1: I BELIEVE THE BEST THERAPY FOR OUR DRESS DESIGNER, DADE PLENTY, IS KEEPING HIM AT THE DRAWING BOARD.

Panel 2: WELL, IF THIS KIND OF PUBLICITY DOESN'T INSPIRE HIM, THEN — THERE'S NO HOPE.

I AGREE, PERFUME.

JAILED DRESS DESIGNER WINS FIRST PLACE FOR ANNIVERSARY DESIGN

.I RECEIVED A PROMISE FROM THE BUYER AT ZEER'S MAIL ORDER THAT THEY WOULD LOOK AT HIS DESIGNS.

THE GOVERNOR IS BEING CRITICIZED FOR HIS PART IN THE REHABILITATION OF YOUR COUSIN, BUT HE'S STANDING PAT.

WHEN I LOOK BACK ON DADE'S PAST, I'M REALLY AMAZED.

BUT I SAY TO YOU, GOVERNOR, YOU'RE LENDING YOUR OFFICIAL BLESSING TO A PURSE-SNATCHER'S FUTURE, WHILE YOU'RE NEGLECTING THE WELFARE AND TAX PROBLEMS OF OUR PEOPLE.

IS REHABILITATION A DISHONORABLE WORD TO YOU, SENATOR?

CHESTER GOULD 8-14-77

© 1977 by The Chicago Tribune All Rights Reserved

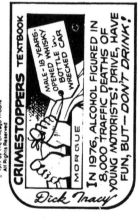

CRIMESTOPPERS TEXTBOOK

IN 1976, ALCOHOL FIGURED IN 8,000 TRAFFIC DEATHS OF YOUNG MOTORISTS! DRIVE, HAVE FUN, BUT—DON'T DRINK!

MALE—18 YEARS. OPENED WHISKY BOTTLE WRECKED CAR

MORGUE

Dick Tracy

I TELL YOU, LYDA, THIS "REHABILITATION" HAS TAKEN A DISASTROUS TURN!

POLITICS! ALWAYS POLITICS!

UNLESS YOU WASH YOUR HANDS OF THIS JAILBIRD DESIGNER, MY POLITICAL FUTURE IS DONE.

From A JAIL CELL

HE DESIGNS FOR THE GOVERNOR'S WIFE

DADE IS A GENIUS AND HE IS DESIGNING ME AN ENTIRE WARDROBE.

130

ONE MORE, MARIE.

OUI?

AND THE MYSTERY TODAY IS, WHO SLASHED THE GOVERNOR'S WIFE'S GOWN AND WHO STABBED THE GOVERNOR?

MY MASTER-PIECE?

CHESTER GOULD 8-28-77

© 1977 by The Chicago Tribune All Rights Reserved

CRIMESTOPPERS TEXTBOOK

ETHEL AND I WILL STAY HERE WHILE YOU'RE AT THE FUNERAL.

THANKS, JIM.

THE GOOD NEIGHBOR PROTECTS YOUR HOUSE WHILE UNSEEN EMERGENCIES CALL YOU AWAY.

Dick Tracy

HATED TO SEE 'EM GO—THEY'RE **GOOD.**

IT'S A CHORAL GROUP THAT SINGS HERE TWO OR THREE TIMES A WEEK. THEY'LL BE BACK.

MEANTIME, REMEMBER YOUR DAILY BUCKET AND MOP DATE WITH THE HALL FLOOR.

LATER

THIS BROOM CLOSET—NOT A BAD PLACE TO CHANGE CLOTHES.

SOAP

—SO THEY'LL BE BACK SUNDAY, EH?

I HAVE A BOLT OF RED AND ENOUGH WHITE FOR A COLLAR.

EASY PATTERN! A CINCH TO MAKE.

9-4-77

CHESTER GOULD

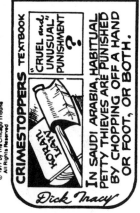

© 1977 by The Chicago Tribune All Rights Reserved

CRIMESTOPPERS TEXTBOOK

"CRUEL and UNUSUAL" PUNISHMENT?

KORAN LAW

IN SAUDI ARABIA, HABITUAL PETTY THIEVES ARE PUNISHED BY CHOPPING OFF A HAND OR FOOT, OR BOTH.

Dick Tracy

SEWING A JACKET TO RESEMBLE THE CHORAL GROUP'S COSTUME, DADE PLENTY MAKES GOOD HIS ESCAPE AND HEADS FOR THE STATE CAPITOL.

YOU CAN'T GO UP, SIR!

THE FIRST LADY IS INDISPOSED AND IS SEEING **NO ONE**-- -UG-UF-NOF-UH---!

ONE SIDE!

SOMEBODY DESTROYED THE GOWN I DESIGNED. I MUST FIND OUT WHO.

While THE MAID PHONES THE HOSPITAL

SO GLAD YOU'RE BETTER, GOVERNOR.

THANKS FOR YOUR CALL, MARIE. GOOD TO HEAR YOUR VOICE.

IT'S ME, MA'M, YOUR DRESS DESIGNER.

CUT TO TATTERS! MY MASTER-PIECE!

I SAY, MA'M--

CHESTER GOULD 9-11-77

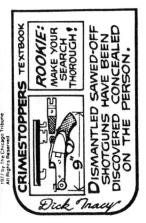

CRIMESTOPPERS TEXTBOOK

ROOKIE: MAKE YOUR SEARCH THOROUGH!

DISMANTLED SAWED-OFF SHOTGUNS HAVE BEEN DISCOVERED CONCEALED ON THE PERSON.

Dick Tracy

1977 by The Chicago Tribune
All Rights Reserved

THAT'S THE WAY I FOUND HER, MR. TRACY. I DIDN'T **TOUCH** HER!

DADE, YOU'RE AN ESCAPEE, WITH A BIG ARREST RECORD ON SERIOUS CHARGES.

YOU'LL BE HELD ON THIS, UNTIL THE CAUSE OF THE GOVERNOR'S WIFE'S DEATH IS CLEARED UP.

Later AT THE MORGUE

IMPORTANT DISCOVERY, TRACY.

"AUTOPSY WAS MOST REVEALING."

FEEL THIS TOP-KNOT OF HAIR.

SOMETHING IN THERE? WHA-AT!!

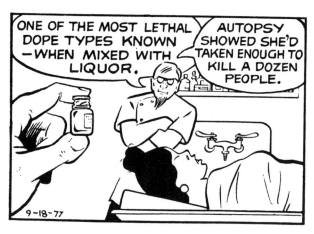

ONE OF THE MOST LETHAL DOPE TYPES KNOWN —WHEN MIXED WITH LIQUOR.

AUTOPSY SHOWED SHE'D TAKEN ENOUGH TO KILL A DOZEN PEOPLE.

9-18-77

BUT WHY WOULD SHE SCREW THE TOP BACK ON AND STUFF THE EMPTY BOTTLE BACK IN HER HAIR?

CHESTER GOULD

© 1977 by The Chicago Tribune
All Rights Reserved

CRIMESTOPPERS TEXTBOOK

SIX STRAYS HEADING EAST ON RAND ROAD.

ABANDONED DOGS OFTEN JOIN A "PACK", BECOMING A DANGER. NOTIFY POLICE OR FOREST RANGERS.

Dick Tracy

NOW, DON'T WORRY, MARIE. YOU AND I KNOW YOU'RE INNOCENT. THAT'S ALL THAT MATTERS.

MR. TRACY TO SEE YOU, GOVERNOR.

SHOW HIM IN, GRIFFIN.

RUN ALONG, MARIE.

IT'S ABOUT THE LIE TEST WE RAN ON YOUR MAID.

AH, YES!

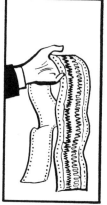

YOU'RE FAMILIAR WITH POLYGRAMS, GOVERNOR.

DID YOU SUSPECT YOUR MAID MAY HAVE BEEN INVOLVED IN YOUR WIFE'S DEATH?

YOU'VE ANSWERED MY QUESTION, GOVERNOR.

1977 by The Chicago Tribune All Rights Reserved

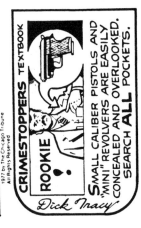

CRIMESTOPPERS TEXTBOOK

ROOKIE

SMALL CALIBER PISTOLS AND "MINI" REVOLVERS ARE EASILY CONCEALED AND OVERLOOKED. SEARCH **ALL** POCKETS.

Dick Tracy

YES, HE TOOK HIS CIGAR LIGHTER AND SET FIRE TO THE POLYGRAM AND LET IT BURN OUT IN THE CUSPIDOR.

AND YOU CAN'T ARREST THE GOVERNOR FOR THAT?

OF COURSE NOT! THE LIE BOX IS UNACCEPTABLE EVIDENCE IN COURT.

HE'S PROTECTING THE MAID. I SMELL A TRIANGLE.

Meanwhile: MARIE, THE MAID, TALKS WITH THE GOVERNOR—

YOU WERE REELECTED! YOUR "REHABILITATION" ISSUE WON WITH THE VOTERS.

AND THE BOY DRESS DESIGNER YOU TRIED TO "REHABILITATE" STILL NEEDS YOUR HELP, GOVERNOR.

THAT PURSE-SNATCHER! WHY HE MAY BE THE ONE WHO POISONED MY WIFE.

YOU OWE IT TO THE MEMORY OF YOUR POOR DEPARTED WIFE TO DO SOMETHING FOR THAT BOY. SHE LOVED THE DRESS.

DO SOMETHING? WHAT COULD I DO FOR THAT JAILBIRD?

PARDON HIM, GOVERNOR.

PARDON HIM?

CHESTER GOULD 10-2-77

1977 by The Chicago Tribune All Rights Reserved

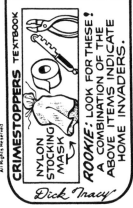

CRIMESTOPPERS TEXTBOOK

NYLON STOCKING MASK

ROOKIE: LOOK FOR THESE! A COMBINATION OF THE ABOVE ITEMS INDICATE HOME INVADERS.

Dick Tracy

WELL, ONE THING HAS WORKED OUT OKAY. THE JUDGE WHO HEARD DADE PLENTY'S CASE HAS JUST SENTENCED HIM TO LIFE.

LIZZ, PUSHING YOU IN FRONT OF A SUBWAY TRAIN, PLUS A HIT-AND-RUN MURDER, PLUS ANOTHER FELONY. THE JUDGE HAD NO CHOICE.

HE SENTENCED HIM UNDER THE HABITUAL CRIMINAL ACT.

AND THIS IS THE CREATURE WHO DESIGNED A DRESS FOR THE LATE WIFE OF THE GOVERNOR!

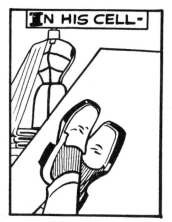

IN HIS CELL—

LIFE? HAH! DO THEY THINK I'LL DIE IN JAIL?

MY BONES WILL NEVER ROT IN A LOUSY CELL.

I'LL—

GET YOUR STUFF TOGETHER. YOU LEAVE FOR THE STATE PENITENTIARY TOMORROW AT 5 A.M..

Scene: THE COUNTY BUILDING

FROM THE GOVERNOR.

WHAT? ANOTHER PARDON?

SHERIFF

10-9-77

© 1977 by The Chicago Tribune All Rights Reserved

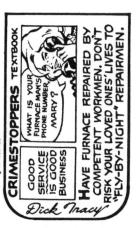

CRIMESTOPPERS TEXTBOOK

WHAT IS YOUR FURNACE MAN'S PHONE NUMBER, MARY?

GOOD SERVICE IS GOOD BUSINESS

HAVE FURNACE REPAIRED BY COMPETENT WORKMEN. DON'T RISK YOUR LOVED ONES' LIVES TO "FLY-BY-NIGHT" REPAIRMEN.

Dick Tracy

I CAME TO THANK YOU, GOVERNOR, FOR THE PARDON.

IT'S MERELY PART OF MY REHABILITATION PROGRAM, DADE. I BELIEVE EVEN FELONS DESERVE A CHANCE.

I'M QUITTING MY DESIGN JOB WITH Da MILL. COULD YOU USE ME AROUND THE CAPITOL GROUNDS, SIR?

A PARDON IMPLIES NO OBLIGATION TO PROVIDE EMPLOYMENT. GOODBYE, BOY.

137

LATER

SHELTER →

CHESTER GOULD

10-23-77

OH, IT'S YOU, MARIE! I HEARD FOOTSTEPS AND --I'M EDGY- I GUESS-

WHAT WERE YOU DOING DOWN THERE?

CRIMESTOPPERS TEXTBOOK

CLINKETY CLANK

PARENTS: CRUELTY TO ANIMALS IS ONE OF THE FIRST SYMPTOMS DENOTING DELINQUENCY.

© 1977 by The Chicago Tribune All Rights Reserved

Dick Tracy

CAUGHT RED-HANDED, THE MAID REVEALS THE SECRET HIDING PLACE OF DADE AND LEADS THE GOVERNOR TO THE BASEMENT FALLOUT SHELTER.

YOU DIDN'T SUSPECT THIS COFFEE MILL LAMP WAS A HOT LINE TO THE CAPITOL SECURITY OFFICE, EH?

I HAD FAITH IN YOU TWO, BUT YOU'RE BOTH UNDER ARREST.

BAM

NOTHING RICOCHETS A BULLET LIKE CURVED WALLS OF STEEL and CONCRETE

CHESTER GOULD

10-30-77

FALLOUT SHELTER

PUSH

WHO IS THIS?

© 1977 by The Chicago Tribune All Rights Reserved

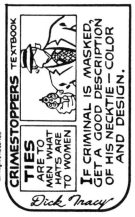

CRIMESTOPPERS TEXTBOOK

TIES ARE TO MEN WHAT HATS ARE TO WOMEN

IF CRIMINAL IS MASKED, GET A GOOD DESCRIPTION OF HIS NECKTIE - COLOR AND DESIGN.

Dick Tracy

138

YES, BULLET SCARS IN THE SHELTER SHOW HOW THE RICOCHETED SLUG KILLED THE MAID, MARIE.

"THE GUN, PROPERTY OF THE GOVERNOR, WAS OBJECT OF A SCUFFLE AND WAS ACCIDENTALLY FIRED."

A HEARING WILL BE HELD ON THE VALIDITY OF DADE'S PARDON.

THE MAID HAD A CRUSH ON THE GOVERNOR AND DREAMED OF BEING MRS. FIRST LADY.

THIS BOTTLE, TAKEN FROM THE DEAD WIFE'S HAIR, HAD BEEN WIPED CLEAN OF PRINTS.

BUT FORGOTTEN EMPTIES IN A CLOSET WASTE-BASKET BORE **ONLY** THE MAID'S FINGERPRINTS.

APPARENTLY THE WIFE ASKED MARIE TO SUPPLY HER WITH DOPE AND MAKE IT AVAILABLE ON REQUEST.

THE MAID'S

IN THE DESIRE TO BECOME THE NEW WIFE OF THE GOVERNOR, MARIE GOT THE IDEA OF A FATAL COCKTAIL PARTY.

CHESTER GOULD 11-6-77

YES, THE FORGOTTEN BOTTLES TELL THE TALE, GOVERNOR.

SHE KILLED MY WIFE!

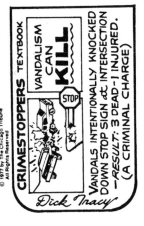

© 1977 by The Chicago Tribune All Rights Reserved

CRIMESTOPPERS TEXTBOOK

VANDALISM CAN **KILL**

STOP

VANDALS INTENTIONALLY KNOCKED DOWN STOP SIGN AT INTERSECTION —RESULT: 3 DEAD—1 INJURED. (A CRIMINAL CHARGE)

Dick Tracy

WITH THE MAID'S DEATH RULED AN ACCIDENT, AND DADE PLENTY ACCEPTING A JOB WITH Da MILL TV COMMERCIAL STUDIO, AND THE GOVERNOR RETURNED TO HIS DUTIES, THINGS SEEM NORMAL AT HQ.

LET'S GO.

I HAVE THE RAZOR.

I HAVE THE SHAVING CREAM AND TOWEL.

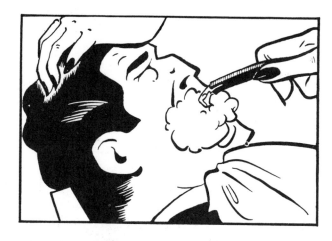

ER- HOW WOULD YOU LIKE TO BE HONOR GUEST AT OUR DISTRICT DINNER TOMORROW NIGHT?

OH- GOVERNOR!

THAT GUY WILL NEVER LEARN.

-SEEMS AS IF!

CHESTER GOULD 11-20-77

1977 by The Chicago Tribune All Rights Reserved
CRIMESTOPPERS TEXTBOOK

WHEN SIREN IS HEARD, OR EMERGENCY LIGHTS FLASH IN REAR-VIEW MIRROR, GET OVER QUICK TO THE RIGHT SIDE AND STOP!

Dick Tracy

ALL I CAN TELL YOU IS, TWO OF MY OLD CRONIES CAME HERE AND WANTED ME TO ASK THE GOVERNOR TO PARDON THEIR BROTHER.

DADE KICKED THEM OUT, SO TO SPEAK, BUT THEY VOWED VENGEANCE.

THEN, PERFUME, WHO WENT OUT WITH THE GOVERNOR LAST NIGHT FOR DINNER, HASN'T SHOWN UP FOR WORK.

Keno FOODS

HMM-M?? HAVE YOU CHECKED THE GOVERNOR'S MANSION AT THE CAPITOL?

YES, TRACY, HE'S NOT HOME.

SCENE: A CLOSED AMUSEMENT PARK-

Y'COZY UP THERE?

YOU PARDONED HER COUSIN, BUT NIXED OUR BROTHER, EH, GOVERNOR? WELL - PLEASANT DREAMS!

CHESTER GOULD

OH, GOVERNOR, IT'S STOPPED.

11-27 -77

© 1977 by The Chicago Tribune All Rights Reserved

CRIMESTOPPERS TEXTBOOK

NON COMPOS MENTIS

A BURGLAR WAS ARRESTED AFTER HE BROKE INTO AN APARTMENT, HID UNDER A BED, THEN FELL ASLEEP.

Dick Tracy

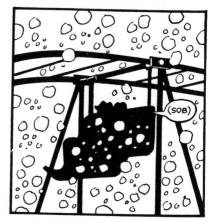

(SOB)

RAIN, SLEET, SNOW! ON A STATIONARY FERRIS WHEEL – IT CAN BE VEXING!

SEE? AT THE TOP OF THE WHEEL?

WHERE?

POLICE

MUST BE PRANKSTERS – I DON'T SEE ANYTHING.

DOTS – DASHES – DOTS – HUH?

"HOW WOULD PRANKSTERS GET TO THE TOP OF A FERRIS WHEEL THAT'S STANDING STILL IN A CLOSED PARK?"

I THINK I READ THE TELEGRAPH CODE SIGNAL FOR S-O-S.

SNOW AND STREET LIGHTS CAN DO FUNNY THINGS, BOB.

YEAH? WELL, I DON'T SEE IT NOW.

BATTERY GAVE OUT!

IT WAS ONLY A KEY RING FLASHLIGHT, GOVERNOR, AND ANYWAY, THE POLICE CAR HAS MOVED AWAY. THEY MUST NOT HAVE SEEN US.

IT'S JUST AS WELL. HAD WE BEEN DISCOVERED – MY POLITICAL CAREER WOULD BE SQUASHED FOR KEEPS.

YOUR POLITICAL CAREER? HOW ABOUT OUR LIVES?

GOVERNOR, I'M BEGINNING TO HATE YOU! WE'RE FREEZING TO DEATH AND YOU TALK POLITICS!

PERFUME! WILL YOU SIT DOWN? THIS ICE IS SLIPPERY – YOU'LL FALL!

CHESTER GOULD 12-4-77

© 1977 by The Chicago Tribune
All Rights Reserved

CRIMESTOPPERS TEXTBOOK

CALL OUT THE CANINE SECTION?

TRAINED LAW-ENFORCEMENT DOGS CAN SNIFF OUT CONCEALED DOPE CACHES and EVEN HIDDEN EXPLOSIVES.

Dick Tracy

DICK TRACY

2-WAY WRIST TV

REPLAY

Y'COZY UP THERE?

YOU PARDONED HER COUSIN, BUT NIXED OUR BROTHER, EH, GOVERNOR? WELL-PLEASANT DREAMS!

W ITH FLAGS AT HALF-MAST, A STATE "BOWS IN GRIEF".

NATIONAL UTELLEM
DECEMBER 11, 1977

WAS GOVERNOR'S FATAL FALL FROM FERRIS WHEEL RESULT OF JET-SET HANKY-PANKY?

OR, DID THE MOB GET REVENGE FOR GOV'S VETO OF CASINO BILL?

The GOVERNOR

PERFUME PLENTY

PERFUME WANTS TO SPEAK.

EASY NOW, YOUR HANDS AND PARTS OF YOUR FACE WERE FROSTBITTEN.

THIS IS THE OFFICER WHO INSISTED THINGS WEREN'T RIGHT AT THE TOP OF THAT FERRIS WHEEL.

"IN TRYING TO QUIET ME, THE GOVERNOR SLIPPED ON THE ICE IN THE FERRIS WHEEL CAR."

YES, PERFUME, THE FALL KILLED HIM, BUT TELL US WHO PUT YOU TWO UP THERE?

IT WAS FORMER BUDDIES OF DADE. THEY WANTED DADE TO ASK THE GOVERNOR TO PARDON THEIR BROTHER.

DADE REFUSED. THEY KIDNAPPED THE GOVERNOR AND ME AND, AT THE POINT OF A GUN, TOOK US TO THE CLOSED PARK. YOU KNOW THE REST.

THE ONLY FRIEND I EVER HAD.

CHESTER GOULD
12-11-'77

Rest in Peace
THE STAFF

AND SO, TO THE MEEK AND THE MIGHTY ALIKE, COMES THE GREAT EQUALIZER, DEATH, AS DADE PLENTY, THE SUBJECT OF A GOVERNOR'S PARDON, BOWS AT HIS BIER.

CRIMESTOPPERS TEXTBOOK

'TIS THE SEASON TO BE JOLLY-

ALSO THE BUSIEST SEASON FOR SHOPLIFTERS! MERCHANTS, INCREASE STORE SECURITY.

Dick Tracy

© 1977 by The Chicago Tribune
All Rights Reserved

Dick Tracy's Family

Dick Tracy really has two families, his police family and his personal family.

Although he asked Tess Trueheart to marry him in the second daily of the strip, Dick Tracy remained a bachelor until December 25, 1949, a full 18 years. However, the strip did take on aspects of a family strip when, as a bachelor, Tracy adopted Junior Tracy, a young urchin in the Oliver Twist mode.

Gould even made a pun when he has Pat Patton, Tracy's sidekick at the time, say, "That's the little dickens that stole my watch."

With the arrival of Junior in September 1932, the strip had a youthful character kids could readily identify with. He was an immediate hit with the public. Dressed in his distinctive plaid knickers, newsboy cap, and with his shock of red hair, Junior was a very well designed character with a unique appearance. Junior also allowed Gould to write into the strip some of the same elements that might appear in a family strip such as "Gasoline Alley." Junior does age in the strip to the point where he's a young man in his early thirties.

The creation of Junior at that critical point one year from the start of Dick Tracy has been attributed to some comics historians as a key factor in the success of the strip. It has always been entirely too easy to think that Dick Tracy is only cops and robbers.

Gould made good use of Junior's trials and tribulations growing up and trying to follow in the footsteps of his idol, Dick Tracy. It allowed Tracy to be shown as a role model for a generation of boys. Eventually, Junior found his niche in the cast of adult characters as a police artist who works with Tracy.

He also was featured prominently during Gould's "moon period." Junior becomes married to Moon Maid, the curvy blond daughter of the Moon Governor. Their daughter Honeymoon is the first child born halfway between earth and the moon on a spaceship.

However, after Gould's retirement, the new creative team wanted to permanently put the moon era behind them and return to the basic pre-space concept of Tracy. The death of Moon Maid sequence contained visually stunning art by Fletcher to accompany the Collins script.

As a widower, Junior later married blond bombshell Sparkle Plenty, the daughter of B.O. Plenty and Gravel Gertie. Sparkle, who in her youth became a television star, in recent years has kept her star quality and in the strip even has her own line of designer jeans.

While Tess Trueheart would come and go in the storyline, Junior played a much more constant role.

However, the romance between Tess and Tracy was a focal point of many of Gould's stories in the 1930's, and Tess showed she could be feisty and courageous. She once tossed Tracy's engagement ring off a bridge during a verbal spat with him, saying, "And as far as our engagement is concerned—well, that's what I think of your little old ring—it was only a half-karat diamond anyway. If you want it, dive for it." This takes place in the middle of a snowstorm in the dead of winter.

Gould claims he woke up one day and just decided to finally marry Dick Tracy and Tess Trueheart. The actual wedding takes place "off stage," as it were, and they appear back in the strip having just been married. Gould explained away this sudden trip to the altar by saying, "Nobody knows anything about love."

In 1951, the birth of the Tracys' daughter, Bonnie Braids, gave Gould the all-American family in his strip—Mom, Dad, and two kids, a boy and a girl. Although there was always a hint of peril in being a member of Dick Tracy's family, Gould did have the family enjoy quiet times together and as a group celebrate holidays such as Christmas.

In recent years, Bonnie Braids, now an adult, has been shown as a school teacher in Washington state on the Yakima Indian Reservation. In 1981, Joseph Flintheart Tracy was born to Tess and Tracy. Believe it or not, both of Tess's children were born in the backseat of a car. It's tough being a mom in the comics.

The mainstays of Tracy's police family over the years have been Sam Catchem, who replaced Pat Patton as Tracy's sidekick, and the police woman Lizz.

It is an interesting fact that Sam Catchem was created by Gould to be a Jewish guy. Gould's agent and good friend Al Lowenthal had suggested a Jewish character for the strip and Gould, who was a Methodist, thought it was a good idea. Considering that this was late when Sam Catchem joined the strip, it was quite an innovative move by Chester Gould. Little has ever been made of it over the years, but it goes to show how Gould's reputation as arch-conservative law-and-order advocate covered over many of the special things he accomplished in Dick Tracy.

Rick Fletcher: The Artist Who Carried on the Tracy Tradition

When Chester Gould retired in late December 1977, he handpicked the artist to succeed him drawing Dick Tracy. The man was his assistant since 1961, Rick Fletcher, an accomplished cartoonist and advertising artist.

Fletcher had been a staff artist with the Chicago *Tribune* since 1946, and since the mid-1950s had drawn the award-winning Sunday page "Old Glory," which was the history of the flags of America and the historical events that surrounded them.

"I drew 'Old Glory' for 12 years," remembered Fletcher. "And I used to bring my work into the *Tribune*, as they used to handle all the comics they syndicated there at that time. It later moved to New York. One day, half kidding, I inquired [of an editor] if Chester Gould was looking for a new assistant. I said that, you know, my wife Beverly wants to move out to the country and I know Chet Gould lives out in Woodstock. Believe it or not he responded that he'd heard Gould did need a new assistant."

The reason for that need was that Dick Locher, Gould's assistant who preceded Fletcher, had for family reasons left the Chicago area.

"So I went out to Woodstock to see Chet with some of my samples and of course 'Old Glory' material," said Fletcher. "His brother Ray Gould was lettering the strip and he had a fellow named Jack Ryan helping out too. Chet at first put me on part time. However, Jack Ryan soon left and I was his full-time assistant. So Beverly and I and our family moved out to Woodstock."

Fletcher was raised in Burlington, Iowa, and discovered as a child he had the ability to draw. He had no formal art training but would spend hours in the local library studying books on anatomy and art.

"My favorite cartoonists as a kid were Alex Raymond, Milton Caniff and Hal Foster," said Fletcher.

"I got my first job as an artist when I was 17 and just out of high school. My dad was upset because I wanted to be an artist. We were a baseball family. My dad had played semi-pro ball and I had a cousin with the Chicago White Sox. I was a natural-born shortstop and very athletic back then, and he wanted me to pursue a career in baseball. But I wanted to be an artist. I should add that my dad worked as a railroad engineer on the old California *Zephyr* when railroads were really something.

"I knew an engraver on the *Tri-City Star* newspaper in Davenport, Iowa, and he got me the crucial interview with the guy at the paper. I was hired as an advertising layout artist and, believe it or not, I didn't know what one did. However, the *Tri-City Star* went broke in a newspaper fight with two rivals, the Davenport *Times* and the Davenport *Democrat*, both of which were owned by the president of the local bank."

After that Fletcher was hired by a local advertising man, Rudy Morritz, as art director. He worked there until World War II began and then joined the Army.

"I was in the Army for four full years," remembered Fletcher. "My unit landed in France on D-Day plus 10 and the Germans shot the heck out of us. We lost half a division in 20 days. This was the 83rd Infantry and I was an officer in the engineer battalion.

"When I went to OCS to get my commission, I thought, Oh boy, I'll be a camouflage officer, as that was a function of the engineers. But at OCS I discovered all the Army wanted was combat platoon leaders. I never did have the opportunity to do any artwork in the Army and often envied the guys who did. The most I ever did was some sketches on the V-mail I sent home. The 83rd Infantry was a hotshot outfit and even Patton praised us."

Fletcher served in five campaigns in the European Theater of Operations and left the service with the rank of captain. He also won a Bronze Star.

After the war, Fletcher understandably felt restless. He returned to Davenport to work for Rudy Morritz again, but wasn't comfortable with it.

"The same drawing board was there in the studio," remembered Fletcher.

Rick Fletcher (left), the new Tracy artist, has a creative huddle with
Chester Gould (center) and Tracy's new writer Max Allan Collins in this
publicity photo released by the Tribune Syndicate in December 1977.

"Nothing had changed except I had just lost
four years out of my life. After the slice of
life I'd seen with World War II, I couldn't
settle down. Also Rudy Morritz was ready to
retire and he offered me the agency. I had
learned a lot from him and we'd worked
well together but it startled me when he
offered me the business. But I'm not really
a businessman, I'm an artist. I debated
and debated what to do. Finally, I decided
to move to Chicago. I had spent a lot of time
there and just wanted a change.

"I had some buddies studying on the G.I.
Bill at the Art Institute and the Academy of
Art and I stayed with them and made the
rounds. The first job offer I received was
from an engraving outfit. Then the *Tribune* offered me a job at $10 a week less.
Would you believe I took the *Tribune* job
because I just liked walking down Michigan
Avenue and going into the Tribune Tower,
which had quite a mystique in Chicago.
That was in 1946."

At the *Tribune*, Fletcher proved to be one
of the fastest and most versatile artists

they had. He did everything from spot art
to advertising work. Back then the smaller
advertisers didn't use agencies and the
Tribune staff did their artwork. His experience gained at Rudy Morritz's studio paid
off handsomely.

Fletcher, who was a gun enthusiast, became known as the best "gun artist" in the
comics. He was also a fanatic for detail and
accuracy.

"Before Al Valanis, an ex-detective,
joined Chester's team as a consultant, Dick
Tracy always used an automatic," remembered Fletcher. "But Al, who always called
Chet Mr. Gould, explained to him that an
automatic was an undependable weapon.
He explained that Tracy should use a revolver. To be able to draw a gun well, you
have to know it and shoot it. I don't like to
hunt, but I do enjoy target shooting.

"When I joined the Tracy team I was able
to arm him with a Colt Special .38 caliber
revolver. However, with a snub-nosed Colt
and a two-inch barrel you don't have that
great an accuracy. That's why, when I took

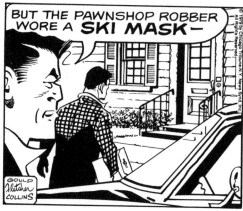

Rick Fletcher always strived to show the latest police equipment in Tracy. The first panel features a new aerodynamically improved light bar for a squad car Tracy shares with Joe Sampson, a Yakima Indian police detective who is the boyfriend of Tracy's daughter.

over all the artwork responsibilities in late December 1977, I armed Tracy with a Colt .357 Magnum Trooper MK111. With the Magnum you can crack the engine block of a car. I also have Tracy use the 12-gauge Model 10 Series B police shotgun."

Fletcher credited Chester Gould for his belief that you really have to concentrate on the task at hand. "Chet lived, slept and dreamt Dick Tracy," he said.

"Chet always wanted to be ahead of his time, such as with the two-way wrist radio, but like any human being he occasionally took a wrong turn. I started with Chet in 1961 and just a few years later he began the moon stuff. I must admit I couldn't believe it when he brought it up. He came up with it right out of the blue. Chet loved the moon stuff and the space program and hated it when the syndicate got on him because they were losing papers over this theme.

And he sort of phased the moon stuff out over time.

"After 16 years of working with Chester, I used to almost be able to predict that he'd walk into the Monday story conference and say, 'We have to have a gun fight.' Or we need some action. Or we need a couple of little kids in the strip. Or we need a little old lady. He loved little old ladies. He knew you had to have human interest and humor in Dick Tracy and was incredibly shrewd in managing to keep Tracy in the public eye all these years.

"Would you believe that every time I draw Tracy I pull out my file and check against Gould's drawings that I have repros on. It settles my thinking and keeps me from wandering from the famous profile. I have a file of all different expressions on Tracy's face, etc.

"You know Gould very seldom switched

A stickler for correct detail, Fletcher illustrated the single-shot stun gun exactly in this story on corporate kidnapping. Industrialist Diet Smith sees both his bodyguards fall.

SOB...

DICK TRACY

Final rough of the character Splitscreen drawn by Rick Fletcher from a rough sketch, in this case both written and drawn, by Max Allan Collins. Splitscreen's scam was video piracy, but his personal failing was an addiction to television. From his wavy lined jacket to antenna eyeglasses, Splitscreen is the complete TV-freak.

hat positions on Tracy, but I have done so just to have a little different perspective to make the art more visually interesting, as we don't have as much action in the strip as we did."

Working with writer Max Allan Collins, Fletcher's responsibility was for artwork only. "I can change the composition of the artwork some, but I have to stick strictly to the script," said Fletcher.

"This is of course quite different from how I used to work with Gould. He started early, about six a.m., and his brother Ray was on board doing the lettering. We'd rehash the storyline and Chet'd ask my ideas. It was fun. We all had fun.

"I'm an action guy and I must admit I long for more action in Dick Tracy nowadays. I know that Chet and I think more alike in regards to justifiable violence in Dick Tracy than the current thinking at the syndicate or that of Max Allan Collins. It's maybe old-fashioned, but I go along with Chet. He'd say, 'The bad guy, you shoot him and that's it.' I haven't killed a guy in the strip since I've been drawing it since Chet's retirement. Usually the most Tracy gets to do is shoot the villain in the arm or maybe the leg."

However, although at times frustrated that he no longer has the input he once did in story conferences, Fletcher did receive a lot of personal satisfaction in visualizing new characters and in presenting innovations in the artwork.

"When I create a new character it takes shape in a number of ways. Sometimes Collins will send me a sketch, such as with Splitscreen. Other times it's up to me," said Fletcher. "Take Poptop for example. I guess he's supposed to be Flattop's father. I just drew Flattop from one of Gould's drawings. Then I made his hair gray and added a wrinkle under his eyes and a pair of Ben Franklin glasses and a super big moustache. That's Poptop. When he opened a poptop can I wanted to get the hand position right and had my wife Beverly take a Polaroid of me opening a beer can so I'd have it correctly. Chet used to have Ray and myself pose a lot so he'd get the action properly. He didn't use Polaroids, we'd just have to hold the pose. But I'm a photo bug."

Fletcher was justifiably proud of his innovations, which he usually features on the TV screen in Tracy's police headquarters. They include: actual mug shots of

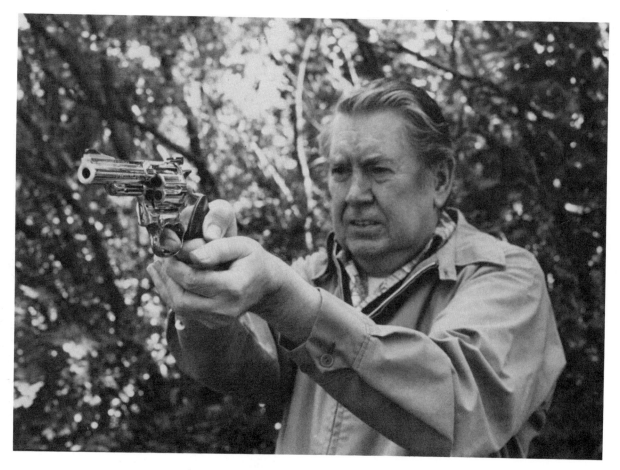

Rick Fletcher aims his custom-made Colt .357 Magnum with Nite-Site presented to him in 1982 by Nite-Site co-inventor Deputy Sheriff Julio Santiago. Fletcher gave Dick Tracy this gun, in his opinion the most efficient police weapon available. (Photo courtesy of Rich Pietrzyk.)

criminals wanted by the F.B.I. and the Royal Canadian Mounted Police, soft body armor for Dick Tracy, police nylon restraining devices in lieu of handcuffs, aerodynamic design for the light-sound bar for police squad cars, and the use of 3-D police targets for firearms training, among others.

The Art Dekko story, about an art thief, included the use by Dick Tracy of the Nite-Site, a device that allows accurate direct fire in low level light areas. Fletcher had read about it in the September 1979 issue of *American Rifleman*, the magazine of the National Rifle Association. He then contacted Collins to fit it in a story. The result made for an exciting conclusion to a Tracy story and garnered the strip an unexpected amount of publicity.

The Nite-Site, developed by Julio Santiago and Elliel Knutsen of the St. Paul, Minnessota, area, uses a radioactive luminous material called prothemium-147 en-

cased in tiny glass beads mounted on the front of the gun barrel and in a bar at the rear. The sight reduces the chances of random firing and the possibility that an innocent bystander might be wounded. Also it allows the officer to shoot to wound instead of kill.

Dick Tracy wasn't the only beneficiary of good publicity from the Nite-Site. The firm making the site received such positive publicity that they presented Fletcher with a custom-chromed real-life model of Tracy's .357 Magnum Colt Trooper.

"Would you believe that 50 rounds for that revolver cost $18," said Fletcher. "But it's fun to shoot."

Fletcher drew Dick Tracy on two-ply Strathmore with a kidde finish, but used the smooth or backside of the paper because of the pen work.

"I work very detailed," he said, "But any kind of felt tip never touches my Tracy artwork. The pen gives me what I call

Artist Rick Fletcher claimed that the Art Dekko story about an art thief was one he had great fun drawing. In it, Tracy uses the innovative Nite-Site, which garnered tremendous publicity for the strip.

accent, others sometimes call it verve, to the line. Making my line interesting to the eye is something I've always strived for. Chester used to use a Gillot #290 pen point, but I don't like to stick to any one thing. I even change intentionally just for the challenge of mastering new equipment. I prefer a Hunt pen point #100 but it's so flexible it doesn't last.

"Rich Pietrzyk rules the borders on the strips and does the lettering for me. I layout how the lettering will fit. After he's finished I start my pencilling. I like a mechanical type pencil with an F lead. However, when I do rough lettering or my layout I use a different type pencil, a plain old 2H. Rich is very thorough and does a nice clean job. He also has lettered for Dale Messick on 'Brenda Starr.'

"I work very clean on the Tracy art and have never used a lot of white out. I think this is due to my advertising background.

In advertising art, your stuff has to be presented to a client by the agency and it has to look slick and clean, otherwise you're not going to sell your product. In fact, Don Michel, my editor at the syndicate, has commented how clean the Tracy original drawings are. He compared me with Leonard Starr who draws 'Annie' and who also works very clean.

"To compensate for the shrinking amount of space some editors give cartoons in papers, I use a different technique between the dailies and the Sunday. I don't use as many heavy black areas on the Sunday because the color will be added. However, Chet used to say, and I agree, that the Sunday should be drawn so that it looks just as good without color.

"Speaking of color, I keep the color on the Sundays very simple. I use a lot of red and a lot of white. Years ago the printing of the Sunday pages was much better. Today you

Following in Gould's footsteps, both Collins and Fletcher felt that Lizz the policewoman was one of the sexiest women in comics. Collins had her kidnapped several times, and this sequence shows how the drama of an empty room can be expanded. "Ye Gods!" is a classic phrase used for years by Gould in the strip. Fletcher commented that his technique of showing a few loose strands of hair to "show action" was learned from the great Chicago *Tribune* cartoonist Carey Orr.

just can't depend on the quality of the printing. I also try to keep my line in the Sunday drawings good and strong to keep it from breaking up in reproduction and reduction.

"In the dailies the key word is simplicity. I attempt to accomplish this with my use of strong black areas. It reproduces well. I do, as you'll notice, like to play with the hair of the characters just to add some action to the drawing. Beverly, my wife, sometimes helps me on inking in large areas so I can save some time.

"I also make a point to include pretty women in the strip and to include some cheesecake just like Gould did. A funny thing on that subject is that my basic research on pretty gals and my clothes for women is the Frederick's of Hollywood catalog. In the Art Dekko story there's a party attended by the so-called jet set, fine art collecting crowd. Every dress and all the furs in that sequence came right out of the Frederick's catalog. It's showy stuff. It's dramatic and looks great in a comic strip. The hairdo for Angeltop was also inspired by hairstyles in the Frederick's catalog.

"I enjoy doing the Rogues Gallery mini-feature in the Sundays, but the one special feature I'd love to start up again is the Crimestopper Textbook that was a staple of Gould's Sunday pages for many years. I think it really got some good information out to people."

Gregarious and outgoing, Rick Fletcher had a passion, other than trying to keep Dick Tracy in the limelight, and it was collecting jazz and blues albums. His portrait of Billie Holiday decorated the front hallway of his home.

In early 1983, Rick Fletcher's untimely death ended his 22-year association with the Dick Tracy comic strip and the syndicate turned to Dick Locher to do the artwork. However, Fletcher's keen interest in keeping Tracy on the cutting edge of technology and the verve and accent of his line will long be remembered.

Max Allan Collins: Only the Second Man to Write Dick Tracy

In forming the new creative team that would take over the production of Dick Tracy upon Chester Gould's retirement in December 1977, the syndicate had a problem. It was a given that Rick Fletcher, Gould's long-time assistant would do the artwork. However, who would do the writing?

The writer selected was Max Allan Collins, a mystery writer in his late twenties. Collins, a comic strip fan since he learned to read, had as a boy written Chester Gould to tell him he wanted to be a cartoonist and to ask if he could take over Dick Tracy when Gould retired.

Although Collins's dream came true it was not by Gould's direct appointment. Rather he was selected by the syndicate staff because of his background as a mystery novelist, his in-depth knowledge of the Dick Tracy comic strip and its mythology, and possibly in part his long-time friendship with Chester Gould.

In 1931 when Tracy first pinned on a badge, writer Collins was 17 years away from being born.

A life-long resident of smalltown Muscatine, Iowa, where he lives with his wife Barbara and their young son Nathan, Collins spent much of his childhood creating his own comic strips, most of them patterned after his favorite, Dick Tracy.

Collins, winner of the 1984 Shamus award from the Private Eye Writers of America for best hardcover novel for *True Detective*, divides his time between writing books and scripting comics. Besides Dick Tracy, he also scripts some of the Batman comic books and his own co-creation "Ms. Tree," a female private eye. His first mystery novel, *Bait Money*, was published in 1973.

As a teenager, Collins' interest in Dick Tracy led to a fascination with the mystery novels of Dashiell Hammett, Raymond Chandler and Mickey Spillane, among others. After receiving his Bachelor of Arts and Master of Fine Arts degrees at the University of Iowa, he wrote *Bait Money*, which in its various editions has sold

250,000 copies worldwide. While at the University of Iowa he studied at its acclaimed Writers Workshop.

Bait Money led to Collin's *Nolan* paperback series. The seven Nolan novels were cited in the anthology *Murder, Ink* as highly regarded "crook books." The series follows aging bank robber Nolan and his much younger sidekick (and would-be cartoonist) Jon, as they seek unsuccessfully to retire from a life of crime.

In the midst of the *Nolan* series, Collins began a second group of "crook books," four novels featuring the laconic, enigmatic *Quarry*, a hired killer whose hardboiled adventures are told in the first person.

The Broker, published in 1975, two years prior to Collins taking over writing chores on Dick Tracy, was singled out by critic/author Ed Gorman as "the most convincing look at a professional killer since Graham Greene offered us Raven in *This Gun for Hire*." Foul Play Press has been reissuing the Quarry novels in paperback and the series has been optioned by Triad for motion picture production.

More recently Collins has turned to hardcover mysteries. His *Mallory* series is published by Walker. The latest is *Nice Weekend for Murder*, published in 1986. The hero is a mystery writer/amateur detective, living in smalltown "Port City, Iowa," and the action is more amiable and "medium-boiled" compared to the tough Collins paperbacks that preceded it. The *Mallory* series is slated for paperback publication by Tor Books.

It may be possible that Max Allan Collins's love of the old Dick Tracy stories of the 1930s and 1940s has led him to his most significant work to date, the historical private eye novel *True Detective* and its sequels *True Crime* and *The Million-Dollar Wound*. All have been published by St. Martin's Press. In these mysteries his private eye Nathan Heller is involved with historical personages and real-life crimes. Some of Chester Gould's early Dick Tracy stories were based on actual crimes in the Chicago area.

Mystery writer and lifelong Dick Tracy fan Max Allan Collins, only the second person ever to write Dick Tracy.

True Detective explores the assassination of Mayor Anton Cermak by (according to Collins) a mob hitman. *True Crime* deals with the shooting of John Dillinger by FBI agents in front of the Biograph Theater in Chicago—although, according to Collins, the man killed was not Dillinger, but a mob-selected "patsy."

The Million-Dollar Wound concludes the "Frank Nitti Trilogy" (but not the cycle of Nathan Heller novels) as Collins takes his private eye to Hollywood in 1939, Guadalcanal as a marine in 1942, and finally back home to Chicago in 1943 as a shell-shocked veteran. The real-life crime Heller explores this time is the infiltration of the Hollywood movie unions by Willie Bioff and other minions of Al Capone's successor, Frank Nitti. The novel explores the circumstances of Nitti's death (long thought to be a suicide—not exactly the case, says Collins) as well as the still-unsolved torture murder of "high-class" call girl Estelle Carey.

Jumping to the other side of the law-and-order fence, Collins is developing a series of historical detective novels about real-life gangbuster Eliot Ness for Bantam Books.

Despite the comic strip field's domination by humor strips, Dick Tracy remains very healthy. Collins feels part of the reason is his emphasis on fast-moving story lines with contemporary crimes such as toxic waste dumping.

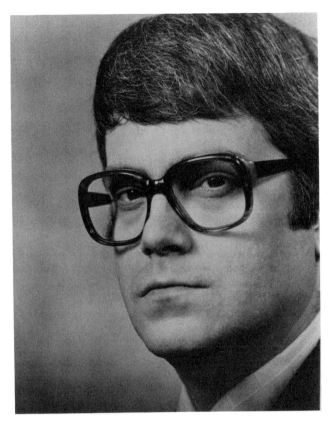

"Dick Tracy works because it is modern, because Chester Gould's original concept was so strong, and because it continues to successfully mix fantasy and reality," says Collins.

"Any so-called science fiction aspect of Dick Tracy I toned down immediately by removing, forcibly, Moon Maid and assorted moon paraphernalia from the strip. But the interest in science has continued with stories about cloning and nuclear fusion.

"Other contemporary stories have involved a love-crazed fan stalking Sparkle

Sam Catchem is shown with Lee Ebony, the black policewoman Collins wrote into the Dick Tracy comic strip. In the last panel appears Collins's possibly most enduring villainess, Angeltop.

Contemporary themes written about by Max Allan Collins for Dick Tracy include inner city arson. His bitchy reporter Wendy Wichel takes Tracy to task as usual. These dailies also introduced B.U. Tiffil, an actress based on Bo Derek. Collins had originally asked Fletcher to draw the famous corn-row hairstyle, but he deferred to an elaborate braid, claiming that he'd go blind drawing all the corn rows.

Writer Max Allan Collins used his 20-year background as songwriter performer with rock bands to create the punk rock villain Bony, who hoped to finance his "demo" record by a series of robberies. His lover Claudine proved to have a heart of gold when she helped Tracy during the delivery of Tracy's son Joe. Claudine even donated her safety pin earrings to the cause.

Plenty, and a punk rocker holding up gas stations to earn money for a demo record; when arch-villainess Angeltop made her first appearance, she was doing the TV talk show circuit hawking a book that "proved" the innocence of her father, Flattop."

The subject of violence in Dick Tracy, too much or too little, has continued to dog the strip as ever, just as it did in Dick Tracy's earliest days. Collins admits that Dick Tracy isn't as violent as it once was but claims he still receives occasional flak.

"The current climate is such," says Collins, "that if bullets went flying through the bad guy's brains, as in Tracy days of yore, we'd lose papers faster than we could count. Still, Dick Tracy is a tough detective strip and there is violence. Witness the hubbub created by that nameless editor near Three Mile Island who—after dropping the strip because the climax of a story had coincidentally appeared the week the

Pope was shot—said that Dick Tracy existed 'solely to perpetuate violence,' and other such nonsense. So what's a guy to do? Like Tracy, I just take my best shot."

During the ten years he's been writing Dick Tracy, Collins has made an effort to humanize the strip. He felt in the final 10 or 15 years of Gould's writing, the Dick Tracy character had gradually become more a symbol (Law and Order First) than a character.

"For this reason I've brought the Tracy family into the strip more," says Collins. "Tess, Tracy's wife, is an active character again, and she and Dick have a new son, who is aging. There have been several marriages in the strip, and the 'family' at Headquarters has been widened to include a young detective, Johnny Adonis, and a black female detective, Lee Ebony. Certain Gould characters that didn't work for me—like Moon Maid and Vera Alldid—were pha-

Collins took the critics of Dick Tracy head on by creating Wendy Wichel, a bitchy aggressive reporter who rarely has a kind word to write about Tracy.

sed out. Others, such as Vitamin Flintheart, I reintroduced."

Collins, who writes Dick Tracy on a word processor, begins each story with a synopsis, a fully-fleshed out short story version of the next Dick Tracy continuity, which is sent to both artist Dick Locher and the editor at Tribune Media Services. Locher will then begin to work up sketches of the "crazy" villain. Occasionally Collins will forward his own rough sketches or photos of actors who resemble his mental image of a villain. While working with the late Rick Fletcher, Collins himself created the image of the villain Splitscreen, the TV addict and video pirate. The fine art thief Art Dekko was developed from a Collins sketch, some Xeroxes of John Held, Jr., drawings and Fletcher's own inspiration. Torcher, an arsonist, came to life from a blend of actors Dan Duryea and Robert Lansing, plus the concept that he resemble a red-headed Satan with his hair a sea of flames and

have some facial features of a dragon, a Fletcher suggestion.

The actual script is similar to a movie or TV script with each panel broken down: action described, expressions of characters indicated, captions, dialogue, backgrounds, and special attention to details. Collins writes the scripts a week at a time, and his deadline to mail them to Locher in Chicago is Wednesday.

"For the first four years, Chet's name was part of our byline," says Collins. "This was partially to assure editors of a sense of continuity, and also because I kept in close touch with Chet and he served as a consultant, though he kept his suggestions general and never worked on a specific story. I would like to see a 'created by Chester Gould' added to the Sunday logo, but that hasn't happened yet."

Collins's contribution to the world of comic-strip detectives does not end with Dick Tracy. With artist Terry Beatty, he co-created "Ms. Tree," a beautiful but tough female private detective whose adventures are published in a monthly comic book. She first appeared in 1981.

As a result of his experience with Dick Tracy and Ms. Tree, Collins was approached by DC Comics to become one of the writers of Batman comics.

"Batman is Dick Tracy in costume hero drag," says Collins. "Robin is Junior Tracy. You know it has all the gadgetry, the villains. They had me write these two fill-in issues and that's how I came aboard. Because of Ms. Tree they knew I could write comic books, because they're not exactly the same form as a comic strip. Bob Kane, the creator of Batman, has admitted himself any number of times that Gould was his primary influence. My first Batman issues were #402 and #403, and in fact DC had me write articles for those issues about the similarities between Dick Tracy and Batman. DC has a commitment from me to write Batman for at least a year."

Collins is also the co-author (with James L. Traylor) of the Edgar-nominated (an award named in honor of Edgar Allan Poe) *One Lonely Knight*, the first book-length critical/biographical study of mystery writer Mickey Spillane. The book was published by Popular Press in 1984.

In the midst of his very busy writing career, Collins also "keeps a hand in" where music is concerned. An off-again-on-again performer/songwriter with rock bands for over 20 years, Collins occasionally provides vocals and keyboards in "reunion gigs" with members of The Daybreakers and Cruisin', two groups he performed with in the 1960s and 70s. Unlimited Productions, a small record company specializing in rock nostalgia, recently released a compilation of tracks by The Daybreakers, who recorded for Atlantic Records in the late 1960s. Collins, who wrote many of the songs on the LP, provided the liner notes.

Searching for a fun couple to be the villains in a story about toxic dumping, Max Allan Collins wanted to use the name Dye. Subsequently slightly modified caricatures of Princess Diana and the Prince of Wales became Dye and Oxen, owners of CIXOT, Inc. (toxic spelled backwards), a firm specializing in illegal toxic dumping.

Dick Tracy's ROGUES' GALLERY

FLATTOP JONES, JR. ARMED ROBBER, MURDERER. ASSOCIATE OF CONVICTED MURDERER JOE PERIOD. SON OF FLATTOP JONES, SHOT and KILLED BY POLICE-WOMAN (LIZZ).

Dick Tracy's ROGUES' GALLERY
FLATTOP JONES

CONTRACT KILLER, IMPORTED FROM COOKSON HILLS TO "GET RID OF, ONCE AND FOR ALL, THE GREAT DETECTIVE, TRACY."
(DROWNED)

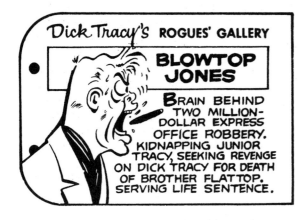

Dick Tracy's ROGUES' GALLERY

BLOWTOP JONES

BRAIN BEHIND TWO MILLION-DOLLAR EXPRESS OFFICE ROBBERY. KIDNAPPING JUNIOR TRACY, SEEKING REVENGE ON DICK TRACY FOR DEATH OF BROTHER FLATTOP. SERVING LIFE SENTENCE.

Dick Tracy's ROGUES' GALLERY

JOE PERIOD

JUVENILE DELINQUENT TURNED ARMED ROBBER. KILLED SISTER OF THEN ROOKIE POLICEWOMAN LIZZ. KILLED "NOTHING" YONSON. ASSOCIATE, FLATTOP, JR.
LIFE SENTENCE.

Dick Tracy's ROGUES' GALLERY

ANGELTOP—A.K.A. ANGELICA JONES

REVENGE-SEEKING DAUGHTER OF FLATTOP. ATTEMPTED MURDERS OF VITAMIN FLINTHEART, TRACY, LIZZ. *PRESUMED DEAD.*

Dick Tracy's ROGUES' GALLERY

MUMBLES—SINGER TURNED CON MAN TURNED MURDERER; HIS NEARLY INCOHERENT SPEECH WAS ENDEARING, BUT HE WAS DEADLY. *DROWNED.*

MM
MMM

Dick Tracy's ROGUES' GALLERY

CHEESE-CLOTH MASK

FRANK REDRUM, a.k.a. THE **BLANK**—SYSTEMATICALLY WIPED OUT FORMER GANG MEMBERS, WHO SHUNNED HIM AFTER A DISFIGURING PRISON ACCIDENT. *LIFE.*

Dick Tracy's ROGUES' GALLERY

MAMMA—GIANTESS WHOSE LOVE FOR DIMINUTIVE ROBBER JEROME TROHS TURNED TO HATE, AFTER HE ESCAPED, LEAVING HER BEHIND. SERVING LIFE, FOR MURDER OF TROHS.

As a tribute to Chester Gould, writer Max Allan Collins created a new mini-feature for the Sunday page, "Dick Tracy's Rogues' Gallery." These examples show the infamous Jones family among other evil doers. The Blank features prominently in the movie "Dick Tracy" that stars Warren Beatty and Madonna. Rick Fletcher's forceful artwork made the mini-feature a success.

THE RETURN OF
DICK TRACY'S

MOST FIENDISH FOE

HAF-AND-HAF!

A new Dick Tracy adventure

RICHARD — WHAT'S THIS I HEAR ABOUT THE SCOUNDREL WHO SHOT ME GETTING OFF SCOT-FREE?

© 1978 by The Chicago Tribune All Rights Reserved

BROMO

SAD BUT TRUE, VITAMIN-THE BROW'S SON HAD HIS CONSTITUTIONAL RIGHTS VIOLATED, D.A. SAYS.

HEY, TRACY! HAVE YOU SEEN THIS?

REMEMBER TULZA TUZON?

HAF-AND-HAF? WHO COULD FORGET THAT FACE...

3-14 78

WELL, IT SAYS HERE HE'S GETTING A FACE-LIFT—AT THE STATE'S EXPENSE!"

NEW FACE, NEW START

Controversial Experimental Rehabilitation Program

BEFORE

AFTER

?

© 1978 by The Chicago Tribune All Rights Reserved

by Fletcher and Collins

165

NEW EXPERIMENTAL REHABILITATION PROGRAM... GOVERNMENT FUNDED...

YEAH! THEY'RE GIVING HAF-AND-HAF PLASTIC SURGERY—THE SHRINKS FIGURE HIS LOOKS DROVE HIM TO CRIME.

FUNNY—I THOUGHT GREED HAD SOMETHING TO DO WITH IT.

READ THE REST, TRACY...

HOW'S THE COLD, LIZZ?

BETTER.

TAKE A LOOK AT THIS, LIZZ...

HAF-AND-HAF'S GETTING PAROLED—DOCS CLAIM A NEW FACE'LL GIVE HIM A NEW OUTLOOK...

BUT...WASN'T HE A CROOK BEFORE HE HAD THE ACCIDENT THAT DISFIGURED HIM?

YES, HAF-AND-HAF'S CRIMINAL RECORD DOES GO BACK BEFORE HIS DISFIGURING ACCIDENT.

YET HIS LOOKS AND A FAST-TALKIN' LAWYER GOT HIM OUT OF THE HOT SEAT AND INTO THE STATE HOSPITAL FOR THE CRIMINALLY INSANE.

AND 10 YEARS LATER WE GIVE HIM A MANICURE, A FACELIFT AND FREEDOM! A MULTIPLE MURDERER...

TULZA TUZON— HAF-AND-HAF— IS A HARDENED PROFESSIONAL CRIMINAL AND COLD-BLOODED MURDERER. CHANGING HIS FACE WON'T CHANGE THAT.

I AGREE. STILL, IF THE STATE SEES HIM AS REHABILITATED, PERHAPS WE SHOULD GIVE HIM THE BENEFIT OF THE DOUBT.

ANYWAY, THE UNVEILING'S TOMORROW.

166

TULZA TUZON –A.K.A. **HAF-AND-HAF,** CIRCUS FREAK TURNED THIEF TURNED MURDERER.

IN HIS YOUTH A TANK TRUCK ACCIDENT LEFT HIM HIDEOUSLY DISFIGURED...

DANGER **ACID**

ACID

THIS, HIS ATTORNEY CLAIMED, MADDENED HAF-AND-HAF, DROVE HIM TO CRIME.

MY POOR CLIENT...

AND NOW, **10** YEARS LATER, AT THE STATE HOSPITAL FOR THE CRIMINALLY INSANE—

IT'S TIME.

90883

DR. CARVER, TO HAVE A "SOCIETY" PLASTIC SURGEON LIKE YOURSELF LEND HIS TALENTS HAS BEEN A GODSEND.

IT'S NOTHING.

"GODSEND" MY EYE–I'D LIKE A CHUNK OF THE CHANGE THE STATE GRANTED THAT QUACK...

GOULD
Fletcher
COLLINS

I DON'T BELIEVE IT—

© 1978 by The Chicago Tribune
All Rights Reserved 3-19
78

AT THE STATE HOSPITAL FOR THE CRIMINALLY INSANE, AN UNVEILING IS TAKING PLACE...

GOULD
Fletcher
COLLINS

© 1978 by The Chicago Tribune ℞ 3
All Rights Reserved 20
78

...TULZA TUZON, ALIAS HAF-AND-HAF...

POLICE PHOTO
Case #321-1928

...HAS A NEW FACE.

HOW DO I LOOK ?

90883

167

SEE FOR YOURSELF.

IT'S A MIRACLE!

TULZA, YOU HAVE DR. CARVER HERE, AND OTHERS— INCLUDING SENATOR BLEDINHART—TO THANK FOR YOUR PLASTIC SURGERY AND THE PAROLE THAT GOES WITH IT.

FINE. NOW, WHEN DO I GET OUT OF THIS DUMP?

HAF-AND-HAF GOT HIS PICTURE IN THE PAPERS AGAIN, GANG— AND YOU WON'T **BELIEVE** IT.

THE '78 MODEL HAF-AND-HAF...

NEW, BUT NOT NECESSARILY IMPROVED

EXPERIMENTAL REHABILITATION PROGRAM PHASE ONE SUCCESS

READ ON, TRACY—WAIT'LL YOU GET A GANDER AT WHAT JOB THE PAROLE BOYS LINED HIM UP WITH...

HAF-AND-HAF'S GOT A JOB AT THE **ZOO**...?

NOT A BAD PLACE FOR HIM.

PAROLE BOARD CAN'T RELEASE A PRISONER UNLESS A JOB OUTSIDE'S BEEN ARRANGED. BUT WHY THE CITY ZOO?

I CAN ANSWER THAT, CHIEF... AND I CAN ALSO TELL YOU WHY IT'S A MISTAKE.

A ZOO ATTENDANT JOB FOR HAF-AND-HAF **DOES** MAKE SENSE— HE HAS A WAY WITH ANIMALS.

GOES BACK TO HIS CIRCUS DAYS.

SAY—REMEMBER THOSE CROWS HE TRAINED TO PURSE-SNATCH?

I REMEMBER, SAM, LIZZ, COME ON... IT'S VISITING TIME AT THE ZOO.

168

YOU'RE GOOD WITH ANIMALS, HAF-AND-HAF — I REMEMBER THE CROWS YOU TRAINED TO PURSE-SNATCH.

PLEASE— CALL ME TULZA.

MR. TRACY, I'M A **REFORMED** MAN. LITERALLY. AFTER MY PAROLE, I PLAN TO REJOIN THE CIRCUS, AS A TRAINER.

BACK TO CIRCLING BROS.?

AND YOUR EX-FIANCEE, ZELDA, WHO BETRAYED YOU?

PAROLE BOARD ORDERED ME NOT TO SEE MY EX-FIANCEE, ZELDA. BUT I BEAR HER NO GRUDGE.

HAF-AND-HAF, WE WISH YOU THE BEST OF LUCK ON THE OUTSIDE... **IF** YOU'RE SINCERE.

AND AS TRACY SHAKES TULZA TUZON'S HAND, A SNAKE IN A BAG SQUIRMS IN THE NEARBY GRASS...

SNAKE IN BAG

TULZA, PLEASE.

I SMELL A RAT.

MAYBE IT'S JUST THE ZOO.

I DON'T THINK SO.

LIZZ, JUST TO BE SAFE... CALL ON HAF-AND-HAF'S EX-FIANCEE, ZELDA, FIRST THING TOMORROW.

TONIGHT, ZELDA, MY LOVE...**TONIGHT!**

YES, ZELDA, MY LOVE — I KNOW YOU'RE IN TOWN.

The Great ZELDA

HIGH DIVER

NO HARD FEELINGS, FOR NEARLY SINGING ME INTO THE CHAIR....

WHY, I EVEN PICKED OUT A PRESENT FOR YOU.

SNAKE IN BAG

170

THIS CAR — AND A MONTH'S RENT ON THAT FLEABAG APARTMENT — ATE UP MOST OF WHAT I STASHED BEFORE THEY SENT ME UP.

SNAKE IN BAG

3-31-78

I'LL NEED DOUGH SOON. BUT FIRST THINGS FIRST.

© 1978 by The Chicago Tribune All Rights Reserved

"FIRST ZELDA..."

GOULD Fletcher COLLINS

SHE'LL BE AT THAT MOTEL, NEAR THE FAIRGROUNDS....

GOULD Fletcher COLLINS

4-1-78

Fair Way MOTEL

WELCOME CIRCUS

ZELDA

© 1978 by The Chicago Tribune All Rights Reserved

HELLO, ZELDA.

Soft DRINKS

CAN'T SLEEP, DICK?

IT'S THAT SCREWBALL, HAF-AND-HAF... MAYBE I SHOULD'VE WARNED THAT EX-FIANCEE OF HIS ABOUT HIM.

"SOME OF THE CIRCUS PEOPLE STAY AT A MOTEL NEAR THE FAIRGROUNDS... I COULD TRY HER THERE."

Fair Way MOTEL

WELCOME CIRCUS

ZELDA

RING

MR. TRACY! OF COURSE I REMEMBER YOU... MAN WHO SAVED MY LIFE! TULZA'S BEEN PAROLED?

SEEN THE PAPERS? NO, JUST GOT IN TOWN. FIRST PERFORMANCE TOMORROW NIGHT.

ZELDA — WHAT'S THAT MOVING UNDER YOUR PILLOW?

MR. TRACY, I DEFY DEATH NIGHTLY IN MY HIGH-DIVE ACT. YES, I'LL BE CAREFUL.

171

© 1978 by The Chicago Tribune
All Rights Reserved

FROM THE BED OF HIS EX-FIANCEE ZELDA, HAF-AND-HAF RETRIEVES A SNAKE...

WHILE ELSEWHERE DICK TRACY WONDERS ABOUT A BROKEN CONNECTION...

ZELDA? ZELDA...?

I WOULD KISS YOU GOODBYE, ZELDA MY LOVE, BUT MY FRIEND HERE SAVED ME THE TROUBLE...

HE'S GIVEN YOU **YOUR** KIND OF KISS— A KISS OF **BETRAYAL.**

BUT AS HAF-AND-HAF DEPARTS...

MR. TRACY... MR. TRACY...? HELP.....

ZELDA! WHAT'S HAPPENED?

TULZA... WAS HERE. SNAKE... SNAKE BIT ME. RINGS... BLACK, RED, YELLOW....

ZELDA? ZELDA?

THAT'S RIGHT...FAIR WAY MOTEL, ROOM 6. CAREFUL...THAT SNAKE COULD STILL BE IN THE ROOM.

SHE DESCRIBED IT BEFORE PASSING OUT—BLACK, RED, YELLOW-RINGED SNAKE. YES, I'M ON MY WAY.

2-WAY WRIST TV

AND AT THE MOTEL...

HOSPITAL? MR. TRACY...HAVE YOU SAVED MY LIFE AGAIN?

ZELDA, THE QUESTION IS: HAS HAF-AND-HAF TRIED TO KILL YOU AGAIN?

I DIDN'T ACTUALLY SEE TULZA IN THE ROOM...

BUT YOU SAW THE SNAKE.

AND YOUR DESCRIPTION OF IT SAVED YOUR LIFE— THE CORRECT ANTITOXIN WAS ADMINISTERED IMMEDIATELY.

UNFORTUNATELY, THE REAL SNAKE IN THIS CASE— HAF-AND-HAF—IS STILL AT LARGE...

MR. TRACY, YOU'VE SAVED MY LIFE A SECOND TIME.

ZELDA, YOU SAVED YOURSELF.

YOU SAW THE SNAKE, AND DESCRIBING IT TO ME OVER THE PHONE BROUGHT YOU THE CORRECT ANTITOXIN.

AT ANY RATE, WE'RE ON OUR WAY TO THE ZOO...WHEN HAF-AND-HAF SHOWS UP FOR WORK, WE'LL NAB HIM.

YOU EXPECT HIM TO STICK AROUND?

SURE. HE THINKS HE PULLED THE PERFECT MURDER.

THAT SNAKE WAS POISONOUS...VERY... BUT THE BITE ITSELF IS SMALL, MIGHT'VE GONE UNDETECTED.

THE DOCTORS COULD HAVE WRITTEN YOU OFF AS HEART FAILURE.

4-9-78

TRY TO KILL ME, YOU LOUSE...TWO CAN PLAY THAT GAME, MR. HAF-AND-HAF...

GOULD Fletcher COLLINS

© 1978 by The Chicago Tribune All Rights Reserved

AT THE ZOO, HAF-AND-HAF RETURNS SOMETHING HE BORROWED...

ZELDA, MY LOVE, YOU ARE NOW BUT A MEMORY...

4-10-78

WHILE, 5 MINUTES AWAY...

ZELDA SHOULD BE OKAY.

IF SHE TAKES IT EASY.

BET SHE'D LIKE TO GET HER HANDS ON HAF-AND-HAF...

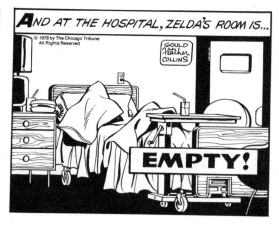

AND AT THE HOSPITAL, ZELDA'S ROOM IS...

© 1978 The Chicago Tribune All Rights Reserved

GOULD Fletcher COLLINS

EMPTY!

A REVENGE-CRAZED, DRUG-WOOZY ZELDA ROAMS THE HOSPITAL HALLS, DUCKING NURSES AND DOCTORS AS SHE GOES...

GOULD Fletcher COLLINS

4-11-78

GOT TO GET OUT OF HERE...GET TO HAF-AND-HAF BEFORE TRACY DOES—

© 1978 The Chicago Tribune All Rights Reserved

NOW THAT IS SERVICE...!

SERVICE ELEVATOR Staff Only

GOT TO GET OUT OF THIS THING AND INTO SOME CLOTHES— HEY!

MAINTENANCE SUPPLY
Hospital Staff Only

AH! A WORK SMOCK...

HAF-AND-HAF...YOU LOUSE... I'M GETTING OUT OF HERE AND GETTING EVEN...

GOULD Fletcher COLLINS

TRAFFIC'S HEAVY, SAM— MAYBE WE NEED THE SIREN.

NO RUSH, DICK. HAF-AND-HAF'S GOT NO IDEA WE'RE COMIN' FOR HIM.

POLICE

BUT AT THE HOSPITAL—

I DON'T EVEN HAVE A WAY OUT OF HERE, LET ALONE A CHANCE OF BEATING TRACY TO THE ZOO AND HAF-AND-HAF...

GARAGE

OR DO I?

GOULD Fletcher COLLINS

WHERE'S MY DOCTOR?

TAKE IT EASY, MR. MASTERSON. YOU'RE JUST HERE FOR A REST....

AMBULANCE

AMB

WHA...?

HEY!

OWWW!

AMBULANCE

GOULD Fletcher COLLINS

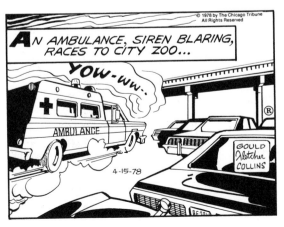

AN AMBULANCE, SIREN BLARING, RACES TO CITY ZOO...

YOW-WW..

AMBULANCE

GOULD Fletcher COLLINS

4-15-78

BUT NOBODY'S SICK— YET!

ZELDA, HAF-AND-HAF'S ENRAGED EX-FIANCEE, IS DRIVING.

NEXT TO HER ON THE SEAT IS SOMETHING SHE "BORROWED" FROM THE HOSPITAL SUPPLY ROOM...

Liquid Drain-X
DANGER!
Avoid Skin Contact

LOOK OUT, HAF-AND-HAF!!

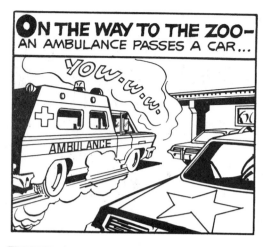

ON THE WAY TO THE ZOO— AN AMBULANCE PASSES A CAR...

YOW-W-W-W

AMBULANCE

...BEARING SOME FAMILIAR FACES.

SAM — WAS THAT ZELDA?

THAT WAS ZELDA.

POLICE

STEP ON IT, SAM! HIT THE SIREN!"

CITY ZOO

AMBULANCE

SQUEAL

TULZA!

ZELDA...? BUT...

BUT I'M DEAD? NO, TULZA. NOT QUITE.

"NOW, ZELDA, MY LOVE," HAF-AND-HAF SAYS. "LET'S NOT DO ANYTHING YOU'LL REGRET..."

© 1978 by The Chicago Tribune
All Rights Reserved

GOULD
Fletcher
COLLINS
4/16/78

REGRET THIS, TULZA!

© 1978 by The Chicago Tribune
All Rights Reserved

ZELDA'S REVENGE!

4-17-78

NOO-O-O-

MY FACE! MY FACE...

GOULD
Fletcher
COLLINS

DRAIN CLEANER... FULL STRENGTH...

TRACY! LOOK!

Liquid Drain-X DANGER Avoid Skin Contact

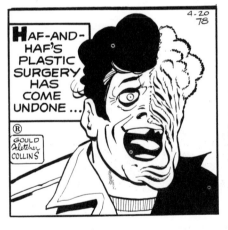

YE GODS!

HE'S THROWN HER INTO THE—

LION PIT!

4-22-78

GOULD Fletcher COLLINS

GOODBYE, ZELDA!

TUZON

HAF-AND-HAF, RESTORED TO HIS FORMER DISFIGURED SELF BY ZELDA, WHO HURLED ACID IN HIS FACE, HURLS **HER** INTO THE LION PIT!

ZOO

TUZON

FAREWELL, MY LOVE...FINALLY, FAREWELL!

SAM, WE'VE GOT TO GET HER OUT OF THERE! LIZZ, TAKE HAF-AND-HAF!

"BUT HOLD YOUR FIRE," TRACY WARNS LIZZ; "TOO MANY PEOPLE TO RISK A SHOT."

HE WENT THAT WAY! INTO THE PARKING LOT!

WHERE **ARE** YOU, YOU CRAZY—

PARK

© 1978 by The Chicago Tribune All Rights Reserved

GOULD Fletcher COLLINS

595

4-23-78

WHILE—

179

YOU OKAY, BOY? NEVER BETTER.

4-28-78

GOULD Fletcher COLLINS

GROOVY, GET HER BACK TO THE HOSPITAL, AND BABY-SIT HER. I DON'T TRUST HER **OR** HAF-AND-HAF...

© 1978 by The Chicago Tribune All Rights Reserved

SPEAKING OF WHICH — WHAT **HAPPENED** TO HAF-AND-HAF? **AND WHERE'S LIZZ?**

© 1978 by The Chicago Tribune All Rights Reserved

LIZZ! WHAT HAPPENED TO YOU? DON'T ASK.

4/29/78

I LOST HAF-AND-HAF. ALREADY CALLED AN **APB** IN ON HIM, ON THE 2-WAY — CAN'T HAVE GOTTEN FAR.

SHOULDN'T BE HARD TO SPOT **THAT** GUY... SHOULDN'T BE...

GOULD Fletcher COLLINS

TRACY HAS RESCUED ZELDA FROM THE ZOO'S LION PIT, **BUT LIZZ** —

BLEW IT! SHOULD'VE HAD HIM!

HAF-AND-HAF NEARLY RAN HER DOWN.

AN APB'S OUT ON HIM, BUT WE GOT NO IDEA WHERE HE'S HEADED.

2-WAY WRIST TV

DON'T WE? HE JUST GOT SPLASHED WITH ACID, SAM — HE'S IN PAIN. HE'S HEADED FOR A —

DOCTOR! GOTTA FIND A DOC AND QUICK...

SHOCK AND RAGE INITIALLY DULLED HAF-AND-HAF'S PAIN, BUT NOW —

NEED HELP! CAN'T RISK A REGULAR DOC, OR HOSPITAL... UNDERWORLD QUACKS COULD BE TRACED...

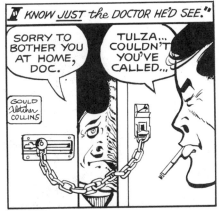

5-4-78

MY WIFE AND DAUGHTER ARE HERE...PLEASE...THE GUN ISN'T NECESSARY.

ANYTHING YOU SAY, DOC—JUST GET ME SOMETHING FOR...

YOU'RE IN PAIN.

THAT'S RIGHT—THIS FACE DOESN'T **FEEL** ANY BETTER THAN IT **LOOKS**...

© 1978 by The Chicago Tribune All Rights Reserved

5-5-78

WHAT IS IT, DEAR? IS SOMETHING...?

PATIENT WITH AN EMERGENCY. I'LL TAKE HIM INTO MY STUDY.

WHAT IN BLAZES HAPPENED, MAN? THAT BEAUTIFUL JOB I DID ON YOUR FACE—**GONE!**

MY EX-FIANCEE THREW ACID OR SOMETHING AT ME—AND THE COPS ARE AFTER ME AGAIN. ANY OTHER QUESTIONS?

© 1978 by The Chicago Tribune All Rights Reserved

5-6-78

THE PAIN I CAN TAKE AWAY—SALVE, TABLETS, THE NEEDLE—THAT'S EASY. RESTORING YOUR FACE, WELL—

YOU MEAN IT **CAN'T** BE **DONE?** I'M DOOMED TO REMAIN A FREAK **FOREVER?**

I DIDN'T SAY THAT. IT'S POSSIBLE. DIFFICULT, BUT POSSIBLE—ALSO **EXPENSIVE**.

© 1978 by The Chicago Tribune All Rights Reserved

HAF-AND-HAF VISITS the PENTHOUSE APARTMENT of DR. WILLIAM A. CARVER...

YES, TULZA—I CAN "FIX" YOUR FACE AGAIN, NOW THAT YOU'VE, ER, BROKEN IT. **BUT IT WILL COST YOU.**

LAST TIME YOU FIXED IT **FREE**...

FREE? HARDLY. STATE PAID ME HANDSOMELY. BUT I DOUBT THEY'LL FOOT YOUR BILL A **SECOND** TIME.

MAYBE **THIS** TIME **YOU'LL** FOOT THE BILL—

NOW, TULZA...

REMEMBER, TULZA—I'LL BE OPERATING ON YOU. A NUMBER OF TIMES. PUTTING YOU **UNDER**—

AND WHO, MY FRIEND, WILL BE HOLDING THE GUN FOR YOU **THEN**?

GOULD FLETCHER COLLINS

GOOD POINT, DOC. WHAT DO YOU WANT?

NOTHING MUCH, REALLY.

© 1978 by The Chicago Tribune All Rights Reserved

"JUST $50,000."

CARVER'S ON THE TOP FLOOR.

5-7-78

HAF-AND-HAF CONFERS WITH THE PLASTIC SURGEON WHO "FIXED HIS FACE" in PRISON.

$50,000? WHAT DID THE STATE PAY YOU, THE OTHER TIME?

5-8-78

GOULD FLETCHER COLLINS ®

LESS THAN THAT. BUT SURELY YOU DON'T EXPECT **ME** TO BE AS BIG A SUCKER AS THE STATE.

© 1978 by The Chicago Tribune All Rights Reserved

IN THE LOBBY DOWNSTAIRS...

CARVER'S ON THE TOP FLOOR.

5-9-78

SO YOU THINK I'M RIPPING YOU OFF, ASKING **$50,000** TO FIX YOUR POOR FACE?

®

IT'S AN INCREDIBLE RISK FOR A MAN IN MY POSITION TO HELP YOU FOR **ANY** PRICE...

"WHY ARE YOU RISKING IT, THEN?" HAF-AND-HAF ASKS.

MRS. CARVER? IS YOUR HUSBAND IN?

GOULD FLETCHER COLLINS

© 1978 by The Chicago Tribune All Rights Reserved

183

5-10-78

I LEAD A RATHER HIGH LIFE—GAMBLING DEBTS, A LADY WITH EXPENSIVE TASTES... MY WIFE'S TASTES, TOO, ARE EXPENSIVE.

I COULD USE A LITTLE TAX-FREE INCOME. $50,000, TULZA— TAKE IT OR LEAVE IT.

"I'LL TAKE IT," HAF-AND-HAF SAYS.

WILL'S IN HIS STUDY. I'LL GET HIM.

5-11-78

SORRY TO DISTURB YOU, DEAR— BUT THERE ARE TWO POLICE DETECTIVES HERE.

YOU DIDN'T MENTION I WAS SEEING A PATIENT?

N-NO...

"GOOD," CARVER SAYS. "TULZA—YOU STAY HERE... I'LL GET RID OF THEM."

5-12-78

IT'S TRAGIC THAT TULZA HAS BEEN DISFIGURED AGAIN— AND IS BACK INTO TROUBLE.

I HAD TRULY HOPED HIS REHABILITATION WAS **REAL** AND PERMANENT.

"THEN HAF-AND-HAF HASN'T CONTACTED YOU?" TRACY ASKS. "WHY, NO!" CARVER SAYS.

5-13-78

IF HAF-AND-HAF SHOULD CONTACT YOU, CALL US IMMEDIATELY. BUT BE CAREFUL — HE'S AS DANGEROUS AS HE IS UNSTABLE.

4308 W.A. Carver M.D.

WHAT DO YOU THINK ?

184

TRACY AND LIZZ HAVE JUST WARNED DR. CARVER THAT FORMER PATIENT HAF-AND-HAF IS ON THE LOOSE...

WELL, WHAT DO YOU THINK?

I THINK HAF-AND-HAF IS IN THAT APARTMENT. DID YOU SEE HOW CARVER'S WIFE AND DAUGHTER WERE ACTING?

WHAT CAN WE DO? WE DON'T HAVE A WARRANT...

SUPPOSE THE CARVERS ARE HOSTAGES? GO DOWN AND CALL IN A BACK-UP UNIT— HAVE ALL EXITS BLOCKED. I'M GOING BACK TO THAT APARTMENT.

ELEVATORS

4308 W.A.Carver M.D.

4308 W.A.Carver M.D.

GOULD Fletcher COLLINS

ELEVATORS

5-14-78

© 1978 by The Chicago Tribune All Rights Reserved

2-WAY WRIST TV

GOING DOWN?

A SUSPICIOUS TRACY RETURNS TO THE CARVERS' APARTMENT AND MEETS HEAD-ON with HAF-AND-HAF...

GOULD Fletcher COLLINS

ELEVATORS

5-15-78 ℝ

© 1978 by The Chicago Tribune All Rights Reserved

AND, MOMENTS LATER, SO DOES LIZZ...

GOING DOWN?

2-WAY WRIST TV

© 1978 by The Chicago Tribune All Rights Reserved

© 1978 by The Chicago Tribune All Rights Reserved

185

NOT CALLING THE POLICE GAVE HAF-AND-HAF A FIVE-MINUTE LEAD THAT COULD COST THE LIFE OF A POLICEWOMAN!

SORRY, MR. TRACY... WASN'T THINKING CLEARLY...

SOME FREE MEDICAL ADVICE, DR. CARVER- PLAY BOTH ENDS AGAINST THE MIDDLE AND YOU'LL END UP GETTING **SQUEEZED.**

NOW IF YOU'LL EXCUSE ME—

IF THAT PLASTIC SURGEON HAD CALLED US IMMEDIATELY, INSTEAD OF WAITING 5 MINUTES FOR YOU TO RETURN TO CONSCIOUSNESS...

THEN WE'D HAVE HAF-AND-HAF IN THE SLAMMER, AND LIZZ **HERE** WITH US...

DR. CARVER'S PLAYING VICTIM, BUT **ACCOMPLICE** IS MORE LIKE IT.

ORGANIZED CRIME UNIT SAYS CARVER OWES THE BIG-TIME GAMBLERS—

TRACY-PHONE FOR YOU, LINE 4.

YES?

MR. TRACY! I HOPE I DIDN'T LOOSEN ANY OF YOUR TEETH, WHEN LAST WE MET...

IT'S HAF-AND-HAF! TRACE IT!

© 1978 by The Chicago Tribune All Rights Reserved

IS LIZZ ALL RIGHT?"

SNUG AS A BUG, MR. TRACY. QUESTION IS — HOW MUCH IS SHE WORTH TO YOU?

BECAUSE I NEED $50,000."

187

5-22-78

A PHONE CALL AT HEADQUARTERS —FROM HAF-AND-HAF!

ARE YOU TRACING THIS?

"$50,000, MR. TRACY... IF THE CITY WANTS ITS FOREMOST POLICEWOMAN BACK ALIVE!

FURTHER DETAILS WILL FOLLOW, LATER TODAY. STAY TUNED...

© 1978 by The Chicago Tribune All Rights Reserved

SLIP THIS GAG OFF—NOW, IF I CAN TIP CHAIR OVER—

HE HAD THIS OLD FARMHOUSE PICKED OUT IN ADVANCE... PLANNING SOME CAPER, PROBABLY—HAD CLOTHES, OTHER SUPPLIES HERE—

THERE!

THUD

© 1978 by The Chicago Tribune All Rights Reserved

NOT ENOUGH TIME TO TRACE HAF-AND-HAF'S CALL. BUT WE DID GET IT ON TAPE.

I NOTED SOME INTERESTING BACKGROUND SOUNDS, SAM.

5-24 78

"MAYBE THEY'LL HELP US PINPOINT HAF-AND-HAF'S LOCATION."

phone

© 1978 by The Chicago Tribune All Rights Reserved

5-25-78

GOTTA CRAWL OVER TO THAT TABLE—GET HIS JUMP SUIT. DIDN'T SEE ME STASH MY 2-WAY IN THE POCKET...

2-WAY WRIST TV

LUCKY FOR ME HE CHANGED INTO THAT FREAKY OUTFIT OF HIS BEFORE HE LEFT— IF I CAN JUST DRAG MYSELF OVER THERE...

...BEFORE HAF-AND-HAF GETS BACK."

THERE'S THE TURN-IN, THERE...

© 1978 by The Chicago Tribune All Rights Reserved

188

WHAT DO YOU MAKE OF THAT?

$50,000... CLANG— CLANG!

RAILROAD CROSSING?

5-26-78

RIGHT. AND **THAT?** BACK THAT UP AGAIN...

...DETAILS WILL FOLLOW. -R-R-**R-R**-R-R...

IT'S A SEMI-TRUCK— MORE THAN ONE! TRUCK STOP NEARBY?

COULD BE. HANG ON, LIZZ— WE'LL FIND YOU.

© 1978 by The Chicago Tribune All Rights Reserved

GOULD Fletcher COLLINS

2-WAY WRIST TV

5 27 78

GOULD Fletcher COLLINS

WHAT'S THIS? EATING BETWEEN MEALS, MY DEAR?

© 1978 by The Chicago Tribune All Rights Reserved

LIZZ'S EFFORTS TO USE THE 2-WAY WRIST TV SHE SMUGGLED INTO HAF-AND-HAF'S FARMHOUSE HIDEOUT ARE FRUITLESS—

2-WAY WRIST TV

"DON'T GET CUTE WITH ME AGAIN," HAF-AND-HAF WARNS LIZZ. While at HQ—

TAPE OF HAF-AND-HAE'S CALL.

SOUNDS OF TRAIN CROSSING AND A TRUCK STOP.

HAF-AND-HAF DIDN'T HAVE TIME TO GET OUTSIDE THE AREA— CALL HIGHWAY PATROL, GET LOCATIONS WHERE TRUCK STOPS AND RAILWAY CROSSINGS ARE ADJACENT.

DICK—JUST SPOKE WITH THE COMMISSIONER. MAYOR HAS REJECTED HAF-AND-HAF'S **$50,000** DEMAND FOR LIZZ'S RELEASE.

I UNDERSTAND... THE "NO HOSTAGE" RULE. I EVEN AGREE WITH IT...

GOT THAT INFO FROM THE PATROL—

WELL, WE'LL JUST HAVE TO GO FIND HER... SAM, I NEED SOME .357 AMMO.

© 1978 by The Chicago Tribune All Rights Reserved

5-28-78

HAVE TO LEAVE YOU NOW, MY DEAR, TO PHONE YOUR FRIEND DICK TRACY ABOUT YOUR RANSOM—

TRY NOT TO JOSTLE THE TABLE—THAT'S A LYE SOLUTION, AND IF IT TUMBLES, YOU MIGHT END UP LOOKING LIKE—

THIS!

© 1978 by The Chicago Tribune All Rights Reserved

A TRUCK STOP, A TRAIN CROSSING, A PHONE BOOTH... THE ONLY SUCH COMBINATION IN A 30-MILE RADIUS, THE HIGHWAY PATROL REPORTS.

THAT'S THE BOOTH HAF-AND-HAF CALLED FROM... IT'S GOT TO BE! BUT HOW DO WE KNOW FOR SURE HE'LL USE IT FOR HIS **NEXT** CALL?

LET'S HOPE HE DOES—FOR LIZZ'S SAKE.

© 1978 by The Chicago Tribune All Rights Reserved

AFTERNOON BECOMES NIGHT. TRACY and SAM WAIT.

WHEN HE CALLS, PATCH ME THROUGH.

← 2-WAY WRIST TV

HAF-AND-HAF IS ON HIS WAY—

ONE PHONE CALL, AND I'LL HAVE $50,000... AND THEN A NEW FACE, FROM CARVER.

AS LIZZ STARES UP AT A WOBBLY BEAKER OF—

LYE!

© 1978 by The Chicago Tribune All Rights Reserved

190

TRACY! MUST'VE FOLLOWED HAF-AND-HAF BACK HERE...

WHERE'S LIZZ?

INSIDE.

LYE

LYE

SOMETHING'S BLOCKING THIS DOOR—

KICK IT DOWN —LIZZ IS PROBABLY GETTING IMPATIENT WAITIN' TO GET RESCUED...

N-N-N-N-N-NO-

I HEAR HER, SAM—LIZZ!

A Rogues' Gallery Reunion

50th Anniversary News Release

In 50 years of comic strip crimebusting, Dick Tracy has made a lot of friends—and even more enemies.

The new creative team of mystery novelist Max Collins and longtime Tracy artist Rick Fletcher—who took over from retiring Tracy creator Chester Gould in late '77—has been making news with their emphasis on modern crime, at the same time creating a new gallery of grotesque villains in the classic Gould manner.

Collins's head-on approach to today's crime problem has drawn fire from some critics who say his explicitness in Dick Tracy could be construed as "instruction" in crime.

"There are some who complain that we teach people how to commit crimes," Collins says. "But you can't tell the kind of stories we tell without the risk that some sick person will imitate it. To me, it's life."

Chester Gould, Dick Tracy's creator, agrees. "You have to keep the pot boiling all the time," he said from his home in Woodstock, Ill. "When it simmers down to nothing, and no one is irritated, you're dead."

But for the occasion of Tracy's 50th birthday, writer Collins—a Tracy fan since age 7—has asked cartoonist Fletcher to dip his pen in a nostalgic well, as a gallery of "old friends" return to plague Dick Tracy in his 50th year.

"One of Chet Gould's rules," Collins says, "was to restrict his villains to only one or two appearances, and he *never* teamed any of them up—a Flattop and Pruneface never got together...which seems kind of a pity."

So, for the first time, Tracy will have a Rogues' Gallery on his hands, as a parade of villains appears in the world's most popular detective strip: earlier this year, The Mole, who ran an underground "hotel" for felons on the run, surfaced as a farmer, no less; and coming up in the weeks ahead are such classic Gould "ghoulies" as Pear-

Logo designed by Fletcher for Dick Tracy's 50th anniversary on October 4, 1981.

shape; Coffyhead; Wormy; Measles; Dewdrop; Influence; and Mousey. Flattop, the most famous Tracy villain, won't be attending this party: like so many of Dick Tracy's foes, Flattop met a violent demise. But his hot-headed brother Blowtop will be joining the festivities.

Pearshape, who was a Chester Gould self-caricature, was a jewel thief who ran, as a front, a mail-order reducing plan; this was a typically ironic Gould touch, as Pearshape *was* pear-shaped. When Tracy tracks him down, however, Pearshape has reformed—literally: he is slim and trim, and the co-owner of a health spa in Beverly Hills, where the Rodeo Drive beautiful people flock to find the secret of this former famous fat man's diet.

Coffyhead, who used an import/export business as a front for a stolen auto parts racket, was seldom seen without a coffee cup (or, at least, saucer) in hand from which to slurp java. Today Tracy finds him as the proprietor of an espresso cafe in San Francisco.

Influence, the blackmailing hypnotist, turns up in Houston, Texas—where, after a religious conversion in prison, he has

turned to aiding the police, hypnotizing witnesses to help them recall details they might otherwise not remember.

Mousey, the beautiful lady shoplifter who would unleash her twin pet white rats in stores and (during the commotion) help herself to the cash register, is today a pet shop manager in Minneapolis—and not at all friendly toward shoplifters now.

This is not to say that all of Tracy's old friends have gone the straight-and-narrow path. Measles, the former dope peddler, and Wormy, a real estate con artist, have teamed up and seem to have something nasty in mind; so does their "moll," Dewdrop, a charming lass who once smothered her pater with a pillow. And Blowtop, who is living in the lap of luxury thanks to the fortune left him by the late Angeltop (Flattop's daughter, a Collins/Fletcher creation), gets livid these days just at the sight of "that cop's mug" in the papers.

And, of course, one of the "reformed" bad guys just may be the "old friend" who sent Tracy a threatening note; or one of the dead villains might turn out to be more alive than Tracy thought.

Dead or alive, it should be a lively party.

Dick Tracy made its debut on Oct. 4, 1931 in the now-defunct Detroit *Daily Mirror,* a *Tribune* paper, and a week later in *The Daily News* in New York, which still carries it. Tracy's pursuit of evil-doers is as relentless as ever, although he deals now with more sophisticated crimes, such things as theft by computer, corporate kidnapping and skyjacking.

"Tracy's ability to change with the times is what has kept him going strong all these years," says writer Max Collins. "Every cop show you've ever seen, from 'Dragnet' to James Bond, comes from Dick Tracy."

Collins's head-on approach to today's crime problem has drawn fire from some critics who say his explicitness in Dick Tracy could be construed as "instruction" in crime.

"There are some who complain that we teach people how to commit crimes," Collins says. "But you can't tell the kind of stories we tell without the risk that some sick person will imitate it. To me, it's life."

Chester Gould, Dick Tracy's creator, agrees. "You have to keep the pot boiling all the time," he said from his home in Woodstock, Ill. "When it simmers down to nothing, and no one is irritated, you're dead."

THE FIRST DICK TRACY SUNDAY PAGE APPEARED OCT. 4, 1931. THE FIRST DAILY STRIP APPEARED OCT. 12, 1931.

CHESTER GOULD CREATOR

RICK FLETCHER ARTIST

MAX COLLINS WRITER

A special portrait of Dick Tracy and Chester Gould was created by Dick Locher for the comic fanzine *Nemo*, which did an issue on Gould.

Dick Locher, Tracy's Pulitzer Prize Winning Artist

Dick Locher's first contact with the comic strip Dick Tracy was as a boy in Dubuque, Iowa, when his dad used to read to him from the funnies about Little Face and Flattop and other characters from Tracy of the early 1940s.

"Dad would linger over the page, looking for the little intricacies that Chester Gould was very good at including in the strip—tiny little things—and my dad was fascinated. Needless to say, all this rubbed off on me," says Locher.

Locher's father told him, "If you can grow up and be like Chester Gould, or like James Montgomery Flagg who painted the 'I Want You' recruiting poster, you'll really be something."

His dad should be proud, as Dick Locher has not only worked on Dick Tracy twice, once as an assistant from 1956-1961, and as sole artist since March 1983, but has had a distinguished career as an editorial cartoonist for the Chicago *Tribune*.

"Although Dad was a dentist, he was very much interested in cartoons," says Locher. "He often talked about things he'd enjoyed in Milton Caniff's work.

"After high school I went to the University of Iowa because Grant Wood was teaching there at the time, but he was fired the week I got there. After that they went into what I considered gobbledygook, with colors flying off in all directions, and I decided that that wasn't for me. Fortunately, I discovered the Chicago Academy of Fine Arts had the program I wanted and its faculty included three professional cartoonists: Ed Holland, the political cartoonist of the *Tribune;* Rick Yager, who drew 'Buck Rogers'; and magazine cartoonist Martin Garrity."

While Locher was at the Chicago Academy of Fine Arts in 1950, a fourth cartoonist, Carl Anderson (not the creator of "Henry"), the assistant to Chester Gould, would appear every Friday afternoon to critique the cartoon students' work.

After two years of art school, Locher left to join the Air Force, where he became a pilot.

"My dad had been a pilot in World War I," says Locher, "and my brother was a B-29 pilot over Tokyo, so it seemed natural that I become a test pilot. I tested extra wheels on planes, heavy bomb loads, ejection seats, new canopies, new wing shapes, etc."

After the Air Force, Locher joined an art studio in Chicago and also became the assistant of one of his former instructors, Rick Yager, the artist drawing "Buck Rogers." Locher did pencilling for Yager and wrote some of the stories. However, the popularity of "Buck Rogers" was slipping, and commercial art seemed Locher's future.

"My debut in commercial art was with Feldkamp Malloy, a studio in downtown Chicago headed by Elmer Holzapfel, who proved to be my greatest benefactor," says Locher. "I was cartooning again and doing storyboards for TV. When I replied affirmatively to Elmer's question as to whether I'd like to have further art training, he sent me out to the Art Center of Los Angeles for a full year with all expenses paid. Naturally he lowered my salary to a minimum, but all my expenses in California he paid.

"At the Art Center I studied illustration, photography, design, art history. In your life you occasionally run across one guy you owe everything to and in my case that was Elmer Holzapfel. His studio had about 70 people and his accounts included Motorola and Zenith. He asked me if I was German and after I told him my name was Swiss, Elmer began to call me 'The Swiss Watchmaker.'"

It was during this period that another cartoon instructor from the Chicago Academy of Fine Arts, Martin Garrity, suggested that Locher begin submitting cartoons to major magazines. His first batch of cartoons was completely rejected by *Look*. However, Garrity urged Locher to persist.

"I then fired the cartoons off to *True*, remembers Locher, "and sold eight of the twelve submitted. I was sitting on top of the world after getting $150 apiece for my efforts. *Argosy* bought my work and then

Pulitzer Prize winning cartoonist Dick Locher, editorial cartoonist of the Chicago *Tribune*, former Gould assistant, and since spring 1983 the artist of Dick Tracy.

mistakenly I concluded that there was nothing to selling magazine cartoons.

"However, *The New Yorker* returned my first two batches but bought an idea, not the art but the idea, which was later drawn by Peter Arno. The cartoon showed General Douglas MacArthur, then chairman of the Remington Corporation, seated at a Remington typewriter with the words on the return key—'I Shall Return.'"

Eventually Dick Locher might have become a *New Yorker* cartoonist but fate in the form of Dick Tracy took a hand. While still at Elmer Holzapfel's studio, Locher heard from Martin Garrity that Chester Gould was looking for a second assistant to help Carl "Andy" Anderson, Gould's assistant on Dick Tracy.

"Gould handed me the script for six dailies and told me to come back in two weeks to show him what I had done. The result was I was hired. What a ball that was," remembers Locher. "He enjoyed hearing me tell about some of his old strips, such as those involving Flattop which my dad had read to me. So one day Chet said, 'Let's do Flattop again.' That resulted in the Flattop, Jr., sequence. Gould was at the top of the heap at that time—at the pinnacle—and it was really fun being part of his operation.

"I should mention that when Chet offered to hire me, I was concerned that after all Elmer had done for me he'd be furious if I left him. However, Elmer told me this was an opportunity I couldn't turn down and sent me off with his blessings.

"I was very privileged to have been with Gould at the National Cartoonists Society dinner when he won his first Reuben award in 1959. And I was proud when the story of how one of the Tracy sequences was developed was told at that awards ceremony. Chet had the theory of putting Tracy in compromising positions for the challenge of it. In the sequence mentioned at the NCS dinner, Tracy was forced to bail out over a deserted island canyon. He grabbed the parachute of one of the thugs, the thug dropped to his death, and Tracy parachuted into the canyon where he spent 30 days trying to get out. He was losing weight

all the time. He was growing a beard. His two-way wrist radio was smashed.

"Chet said to me, 'How are we going to get him out of here? Come in with some suggestions next Monday.' On Monday, which was our regular writing day, I said, 'We're right in the middle of the Army missile peak. Why don't we have a wayward missile drift into the canyon, followed by a bevy of helicopters?' Chet said, 'Yeah—that's a good story, that'll make them sit up and take notice.'

"Chester Gould was one of the people who could take a two-dimensional art form and turn that into the most glorious hunk of entertainment you could imagine."

In 1961, Dick Locher's father died and family responsibilities prevented him from continuing as a Gould assistant. He returned to commercial art.

In 1962, Locher started his own commercial art studio which he kept open 10 years. His best client was McDonald's Hamburgers for whom he designed some of the characters familiar to millions of kids. Other clients included Coca-Cola, Beech Aircraft, John Deere, US Steel, and Cessna Aircraft. His firm, Noramark Corporation, was located in suburban Oak Brook, Illinois, outside Chicago.

Throughout his life, Locher had kept an interest in editorial cartoons, occasionally sketching some just for his own amusement. This proved more than helpful when out of the blue his old friend Chester Gould called him up and told him that the editorial cartoonist position at the Chicago *Tribune* was opening up.

"Chet called me and said, 'Would you be interested in doing some editorial cartoons for the Chicago *Tribune*?'" remembers Locher. "He told me the *Tribune* had a mandatory retirement at age 65 and that Joe Parrish, the editorial cartoonist, was going to leave. Gould said, 'Get 12 cartoons and get down there tomorrow afternoon.' I said, 'I've never done any professionally before.' To which he replied, 'That doesn't make any difference—do 12 and get down there.'"

Dick Locher was hired by the Chicago *Tribune* and in April 1983, just five days short of his tenth anniversary with the *Tribune*, won the Pulitzer Prize for cartooning. The cartoons that earned him the award touched on topics from President Reagan to the Middle East to home computers. Locher's work currently appears on both the *Tribune's* editorial and op-ed pages.

His editorial cartoons are nationally syndicated by Tribune Media Services and have been reprinted in *Time*, *Newsweek*, *U.S. News and World Report*, *Harvard Business Review*, *Forbes*, *Playboy*, and many other publications. Two collections of his editorial cartoons have been published, *Dick Locher Draws Fire* (1979) and *Send in the Clowns* (1982). He also collaborated with *Tribune* columnist Michael Killian on the book *Flying Can be Fun* in 1985.

Locher's awards for his editorial work are numerous. In 1983 and 1984, he won first place in the Overseas Press Club competition. And in 1985, Locher won the Distinguished Health Journalism Award for the fifth time. He has also been honored by Sigma Delta Chi and the Society of Professional Journalists.

In editorial cartooning, Locher maintains that the "idea is king." He says that his best ideas come from conversations with others, when they really let you know what they feel about the world situation.

For about ten years Locher concentrated his talents just on editorial cartooning. Then in 1983 he took on two additional jobs, first "Clout St.," and then Dick Tracy.

"In late 1977, Chester Gould retired from

One of the cartoons Dick Locher received the Pulitzer Prize for.

Country bumpkin B.O. Plenty chews tobacco and doesn't believe in banks. The character was created by Gould to add humor to the strip and was based on a type of rough-around-the-edges country boy Gould knew in his Oklahoma youth. Writer Max Collins captures B.O.'s encounter with the IRS in a traditional Gould way. Artist Dick Locher has stated that he desires to keep the Gould flavor in the strip.

Dick Tracy," says Locher, "and Max Allan Collins and Rick Fletcher took over doing the strip. Then, unfortunately, in March 1983, Fletcher passed away. A month prior to that, my editor at the *Tribune*, Jim Squires, who was lamenting the loss of 'Doonesbury' during Gary Trudeau's sabbatical, said, 'We could really use another strip like that—would anyone be interested in trying one?' Jeff MacNelly, who was at the *Tribune* at the time, and I said, 'Why not.' So "Clout St." was born in February 1983."

In having Jeff MacNelly as co-creator of Clout St., Locher had hooked in with a two-time winner of both the Pulitzer Prize for editorial cartooning and the Cartoon Society's Reuben Award for Cartoonist of the Year. MacNelly's humor comic strip "Shoe" is syndicated in over 700 newspapers.

Clout St. was a satirical strip based on the type of political buffoons found in any

city, large or small. The mayor is never shown. His word balloons are issued from the imposing highbacked executive chair shown in sillouette. Or the mayor's words are shown coming from the back of his limo. His right-hand man is his press secretary McGuff.

There's a bag lady, who has turned out to be the star of the strip, who comments on the city scene and is against anything the city comes out with. Her foil is often Officer Biff Seidensticker, who's on the take.

When Clout St. first began it was drawn as daily strips only, but printed in color in the *Tribune*, which is quite unusual. The strip did become nationally syndicated, but its success seems destined to be regional to the Chicago area.

Originally Cloud St. was signed by Locher and MacNelly; both are no longer associated with the strip, which is now signed "Tribs" to represent a group of writ-

ers and artists from the Chicago *Tribune.* Locher's involvement ceased in 1984 due to the workload.

"Jeff and I had been doing Clout St. for about a month," remembers Locher, "when I had a call from Bob Reed, the President of the Tribune Syndicate. He asked me if I would be interested in drawing Dick Tracy? He also needed an almost immediate response as Fletcher's illness had been sudden and the syndicate didn't have that much lead time.

"I tried to explain I was pretty involved with the combination of my editorial cartooning and the new Clout St. strip. But Bob Reed persisted and I agreed to give Dick Tracy a try. So there I was in March 1983 with responsibility for the artwork on Dick Tracy, Clout St. and five editorial

cartoons a week. Then on top of that, one month later I won the Pulitzer Prize. I can remember my editor saying, 'Now you've really got to be good because everybody'll be watching.'

"But we sailed into it and, with Mac-Nelly's help and editor Squires' input on the script for Clout St., we got by. Jeff would sketch, I would ink. Then I would sketch and Jeff would ink. It was wild.

"As for Dick Tracy, the scripts were mailed to me by Max Allan Collins from his home in Muscatine, Iowa. And every week I'd pencil like crazy to get everything done. So I ended up with your basic 65-hour work week. After awhile the bags under the eyes started to show and my editor, Jim Squires, suggested I look for an assistant.

"Well the cavalry was on the way in the

"COME OUT! I KNOW YOU'RE IN THERE!!"

Dick Locher and writer Max Allan Collins continue the tradition of a special Christmas daily in which they have the main characters of the strip give their readers holiday greetings.

form of my son, John Locher, who graduated from Northern Illinois University in DeKalb, Illinois, with a degree in Fine Arts in June 1983."

The team of Locher and Locher worked beautifully together from the start. Fresh from college, John Locher was thrilled to be working on Dick Tracy, and had the enthusiasm of youth. He did backgrounds, figures, sketching, reworking panels, and a little bit of everything in assisting his dad.

"When I took over Dick Tracy's artwork," says Locher, "the theory was that I would gradually ease into my style—which I think I've done—but I'm trying to emulate Gould as much as possible because I think there's a younger generation reading the strip now which has never seen the way Gould did it—which was masterful. The use of black areas, the balance, the perspective and the depth that he would put into a panel, was just unbeatable. I'm nowhere near that, but my son John and I strive for that goal."

Collins and Locher have a good working relationship, and when Dick Locher suggested a white-collar Yuppie criminal, Collins responded with the Upwardly Mobile story reprinted in this volume.

Until Chester Gould's death in May 1985, Locher especially enjoyed their monthly lunches at Chicago's Tavern Club. They'd meet at noon and the lunches lasted well into the afternoon. Chester still maintained an office in the Tribune Tower, a Chicago landmark.

"One time we had to draw a machine gun," remembers Locher. "Chet says to me that there's one in the closet in his office. Then he encouraged me to wrap it up in a bag and take it home to sketch from. The gun had a clip in it but no bullets and a police tag on it, so I assume he had borrowed it from the police department.

"As I left the Tribune Tower and was walking toward Union Station, I felt that I was being watched. Shortly I was stopped by two Chicago policemen. The officers asked what I had in the package and I responded that it was leftover pizza and I was in a hurry to catch my train home. They asked to see the leftover pizza? At this point I felt pretty silly and decided to face up to the truth and take what was coming to me. I unwrapped the gun.

" 'Sir, you know you can't carry a machine gun around the streets of Chicago—

Lizz the policewoman, who often has her name incorrectly shortened to one "z" by comics historians, was a character created by Gould to try and interest women into reading Dick Tracy.

With Tracy married and totally faithful to his beloved Tess, Lizz also provided romantic interest. Her hot-and-cold love affair with police officer Groovy Grove began in 1971 and ended with her marriage to Groovy in 1984 at his deathbed.

Lizz was successfully used by both Gould and Fletcher to bring an incredible amount of sexuality to the strip. The Gould strip above shows how he used the era of the mini-skirt to catch his male readers' glance.

In recent years, Lee Ebony, a black policewoman, has joined Lizz as part of the Dick Tracy team.

Artist Dick Locher has drawn Chester Gould as the minister who marries Lizz and Groovy.

that's totally against the law and we're going to have to take you downtown,' said one officer. Then they started to laugh. It seems Gould had called the police department as a joke and told them I was coming out of the building with a machine gun in the package.

In drawing Dick Tracy the artwork is done on 2-ply Strathmore with as much of it as possible being done with a #4 Windsor-Newton watercolor brush. Of course, some is inked in with pen. Locher is not fussy about what he uses for penciling and claims to use "whatever is lying around."

"For the reason that many papers reproduce Dick Tracy and all their comic strips are so small, you can't put the amount of detail in that Chet used to in the old days or even when I assisted him," says Locher. "In fact, the drawings for Tracy I did in 1983 when I started are bigger than the ones I'm drawing now. Currently Tracy on Sunday is offered to newspapers as a full tabloid size, a half page format and the quarter and third page formats.

"For researching the strip, I must comment that Max Allan Collins is very thorough in sending me photos, sketches, etc. Also, here in Chicago, which has such a rich tradition of association with Dick Tracy, I have an open conduit to help from the Chicago Police Department. Women's fashion I take from the Marshall Field catalog."

In May of 1986, tragedy struck the creative team producing Dick Tracy; without warning, 25-year-old John Locher was overcome by a seizure and died. John had just completed a full day's work at the drawing board on Tracy. The suddenness of the tragedy heightened the loss for his parents.

Ray Shlemon, a retired Chicago *Tribune* staff artist, is now assisting Dick Locher with the artwork for Dick Tracy. Ray who has a great deal of experience in police reporting, also helps Locher research the details of police procedure so vital to the authenticity of the strip.

Dick Locher is very much a family man who feels that he owes a lot to his wife, Mary. They have another son, Steve, and a daughter, Jana.

"Mary's put up with more than anyone can imagine," he says. "She's put up with extra work, extra time, extra hours, and even helped me pencil a few times when I was under the gun."

1961   1986

John Locher

Portrait of John Locher (1961-1986), drawn by his father Dick Locher. John assisted his father on the artwork for Dick Tracy from late spring 1983 until his untimely death in 1986.

You're in Good Hands with Uppward Lee-Mobile

by Locher and Collins

DO YOU REALIZE YOU'VE JUST ALLOWED $1,000,000 TO WALK OUT THAT DOOR?

QUIET, MY SWEET...

YOUR LITTLE TRENDY ISN'T **COMPUTER LITERATE** FOR NOTHING — AH! JUST AS I THOUGHT...

NO LIVING RELATIVES...

STRONG W

© 1986 Tribune Media Services, Inc. All Rights Reserved

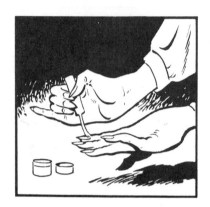

Every MORNING, BUSINESS EXECUTIVE **WALTER STRONG** GOES OUT JOGGING — THIS MORNING HE'S ABOUT TO HAVE SOME **COMPANY** —

WELL, MS. LEE-MOBILE! I'VE NEVER SEEN **YOU** OUT RUNNING IN THE PARK, BEFORE —

MY AEROBICS INSTRUCTOR RECOMMENDED IT — AND CALL ME **TRENDY**.

YOU'LL BE GLAD TO KNOW YOUR MILLION-DOLLAR CHECK IS ALREADY WAITING FOR YOU AT OUR OFFICE, MR. STRONG.

CALL ME WALTER. SORRY I GOT HOT UNDER THE COLLAR YESTERDAY —

THAT'S OKAY — OOWW!!

WHAT'S WRONG?

GUESS I'M NOT USED TO THIS — LEG CRAMPED UP ON ME.

LET ME MASSAGE IT — WORK IT OUT —

YOU'RE VERY KIND —

© 1986 Tribune Media Services, Inc. All Rights Reserved

OUCH!

SORRY! THESE DARNED **NAILS** OF MINE...

WALTER STRONG... DEAD! WHY, HE WAS IN BETTER SHAPE THAN ANY MAN I KNOW!

"HE HAS NO HISTORY OF HEART TROUBLE— HE HAD A COMPANY PHYSICAL JUST A FEW **MONTHS** AGO..."

"DIET, LET'S GO TO THAT HOSPITAL. I'D LIKE A LOOK AT STRONG'S BODY."

WHY DID YOU **DO** IT?

FOR THE MONEY.

3·4

YOU KILLED STRONG FOR THE **MONEY**? WE COULD'VE AFFORDED TO GIVE HIM THE DOUGH!

YOU HAVEN'T CHECKED THE BOOKS LATELY, UPPWARD DEAR—THE **REAL** BOOKS.

3·5

"FIVE HOMES, TWO JETS AND A DOZEN CARS DON'T COME **CHEAP**, YOU KNOW."

WALTER STRONG? RIGHT THIS WAY, DETECTIVE TRACY—

WE'VE BEEN PAYING OFF OUR EARLY INVESTORS, TO PUT A GOOD FACE ON THINGS—

"NOT TO **MENTION** OUR CHARITABLE AND POLITICAL CONTRIBUTIONS."

"IT'S ALL TAKEN A **FINANCIAL** TOLL!"

HEART ATTACK, DETECTIVE.

THAT'S NOT **MY** DIAGNOSIS, DOCTOR.

MY FRIEND DIET SMITH IS A STONE **HEALTH** FREAK— HIS COMPANY'S PHYSICALS ARE COMPLETE AND RIGOROUS—

3·7

AND THIS MAN JUST PASSED WITH FLYING COLORS— **HEY!**

"WHAT'S THIS **SCRATCH** ON HIS NECK?"

WE SIMPLY COULDN'T **AFFORD** PAYING STRONG.

PERHAPS YOU'RE RIGHT— BUT KILLING SEEMS SO... **EXTREME**, SOMEHOW.

THIS SCRATCH IS ALMOST AN **INCISION** - AND A **RECENT** ONE, AT THAT -

WHAT - ?

I REQUESTED AN AUTOPSY.

© 1986 Tribune Media Services, Inc. All Rights Reserved

" I SUSPECT YOUR FRIEND WALTER STRONG IS A **MURDER** VICTIM."

3·8

STRONG'S DEATH HAS BEEN ACCEPTED AS A HEART ATTACK!

I TOLD YOU, LOVE. TRUST YOUR LITTLE TRENDY.

SWEATS AND TENNIES - WHAT SORT OF WAY IS **THIS** TO START THE DAY ?

WHAT'S THE OCCASION? NEW DEPARTMENTAL FITNESS PROGRAM?

SAME OLD PROGRAM - CATCHING CROOKS - **MURDERERS**.

DIET'S FRIEND WALTER STRONG WAS **KILLED** - POISONED, ACCORDING TO THE AUTOPSY REPORT.

"BUT HE DIED OF A **HEART ATTACK**," SAM SAYS, "RIGHT HERE AT THE PARK - WHICH IS JUST **ANOTHER** REASON I AIN'T INTERESTED IN JOGGING!"

3·9

"DON'T BELIEVE EVERYTHING YOU READ IN THE PAPERS," TRACY SAYS. "STRONG WAS EXPOSED TO A FAST-ACTING WEST INDIAN POISON, THE AFTERMATH OF WHICH IS OFTEN MISTAKEN FOR A HEART ATTACK."

HE WAS SCRATCHED OR CUT ON THE NECK - PROBABLY HERE IN THE PARK. SHOW THESE AROUND -

NO.

NO.

YES!

© 1986 Tribune Media Services, Inc. All Rights Reserved

I SURE **DO** RECOGNIZE HIM— THAT'S THE JOGGER WHO KEELED OVER THE OTHER DAY!

3·10

I'M THE ONE WHO CALLED FOR AN AMBULANCE—

IMAGINE A HEALTHY-LOOKING GUY LIKE THAT DROPPING DEAD—" "**MURDER'LL** DO THAT," TRACY SAYS.

"DIED OF A HEART ATTACK, WHILE **JOGGING**..."

NO PAIN, NO GAIN.

© 1986 Tribune Media Services, Inc. All Rights Reserved

DICK LOCHER MAX COLLINS

HIS NAME WAS **WALTER STRONG**— AND HE **DIDN'T** DIE OF A HEART ATTACK.

DICK LOCHER MAX COLLINS

A RARE WEST INDIAN POISON WAS INTRODUCED INTO HIS SYSTEM **MINUTES** BEFORE YOU SAW HIM FALL.

3·11

© 1986 Tribune Media Services, Inc. All Rights Reserved

"**D**ID YOU SEE ANYONE WITH STRONG BEFORE HE DIED?"

PENCIL ME IN FOR LUNCH, DEAR— I'M OFF TO MY THERAPY SESSION—

LIZZ, TAKE MR. JEROGG TO HEADQUARTERS AND HAVE JUNIOR WORK UP A SKETCH OF THE WOMAN SEEN JOGGING WITH STRONG.

3·13 ®

WHAT ABOUT US?

WE'RE GOING TO PUT ON OUR BEST DESIGNER PLAINCLOTHES—

© 1986 Tribune Media Services, Inc. All Rights Reserved

"**A**ND VISIT THE LATE MR. STRONG'S FINANCIAL ADVISER **UPPWARD LEE-MOBILE.**"

DICK LOCHER MAX COLLINS

DO WE HAVE A DESCRIPTION OF THE WOMAN SEEN WITH WALTER STRONG?

YES—

3·15 DICK LOCHER MAX COLLINS ®

"**B**UT SHE SOUNDS PRETTY ORDINARY: AN ATTRACTIVE BLONDE OF ABOUT 25."

THAT'S CLOSE—

© 1986 Tribune Media Services, Inc. All Rights Reserved

"**I**S THERE ANYTHING ELSE **DISTINCTIVE** YOU CAN REMEMBER?" JUNIOR ASKS.

UPPWARD LEE-MOBILE? POLICE. A FEW QUESTIONS...

THAT'S VERY GOOD- BUT HER HAIR SORT OF FLIPS OVER TO ONE SIDE.

OKAY...

WHILE POLICE ARTIST JUNIOR WORKS UP A SKETCH OF THE FEMALE JOGGER SEEN WITH WALTER STRONG, TRACY AND SAM GO CALLING ON -

UPPWARD LEE-MOBILE, GENTLEMEN! WELCOME TO MY WORKING SPACE.

IT'S AN HONOR INTERFACING WITH THE FAMOUS DETECTIVE TRACY.

THANKS. ISN'T YOUR WIFE YOUR BUSINESS PARTNER?

"YES, BUT SHE'S IN THERAPY THIS MORNING - THREE MORNINGS A WEEK, ACTUALLY."

I UNDERSTAND THE LATE WALTER STRONG WAS YOUR CLIENT-

ER, UH - YES. WE WERE WORLD-CLASS FRIENDS, WALTER AND I - HIS DEATH IS A TRAGIC LOSS.

CAN I HAVE MY SECRETARY GET YOU SOME CAPPUCINO, GENTLEMEN?

NEVER TOUCH THE STUFF. WHAT WE'RE INTERESTED IN IS YOUR FINANCIAL DEALINGS WITH MR. STRONG -

DICK LOCHER MAX COLLINS ®

1986 Tribune Media Services, Inc. All Rights Reserved

ACHING AEROBICS! HOW DARE YOU MAKE SUCH WILD ACCUSATIONS!

3-16.

DITHERING DIVESTITURES! STRONG WITHDREW HIS INVESTMENTS WITH US!

® DICK LOCHER MAX COLLINS

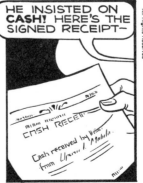

HE INSISTED ON CASH! HERE'S THE SIGNED RECEIPT-

© 1986 Tribune Media Services, Inc. All Rights Reserved

IF THE MONEY IS MISSING, WHY I'M SURE I DON'T KNOW ABOUT IT-

3-19

YOU DON'T MIND IF WE TAKE THIS RECEIPT FOR WALTER STRONG'S **MILLION?**

CERTAINLY NOT. I HAVE A PHOTOCOPY FOR MY RECORDS.

3·20 ®

© 1986 Tribune Media Services, Inc. All Rights Reserved

THANKS FOR YOUR COOPERATION, MR. LEE-MOBILE—WE DIDN'T MEAN TO **UPSET** YOU—

UPSET ME? WHY, I ALWAYS STAY COOL AS A KIWI, DETECTIVE.

DICK LOCHER
MAX COLLINS

YOU LOOK TRIM FOR A MAN YOUR AGE, DETECTIVE TRACY—

I WORK OUT WHEN I CAN—

DICK LOCHER
MAX COLLINS

3·22 ®

"UT I CAN'T AFFORD A HEALTH CLUB AND THE POLICE GYM GETS PRETTY CROWDED."

© 1986 Tribune Media Services, Inc. All Rights Reserved

I HAVE A PRIVATE GYM AT MY LIVING SPACE— FEEL FREE TO DROP BY, ANYTIME—YOU'LL **LOVE** IT—

DICK TRACY WAS HERE?

NOT TO WORRY. I GAVE HIM **ZILCH**—

LEE, TAKE THIS COPY OF OUR **SUSPECT** SKETCH TO THE PARK TOMORROW MORNING—

AND RUN IT PAST THE JOGGERS? CHECK!

HOW DID **UPPWARD LEE-MOBILE** TAKE TO BEING INTERROGATED?

"HE REACTED TO 'HOW ARE YA' LIKE IT WAS AN ACCUSATION!" SAM SAYS.

I TELL YA, TRACY, THAT GUY'S GUILTY OF **SOMETHING!**

HE **IS** VOLATILE—

VOLATILE? THAT GUY'S A CUISINART ON **OVERDRIVE!**

WHAT ABOUT THE BUSINESS PARTNER/ WIFE?

"SHE WAS AT HER ANALYST," TRACY SAYS. "WE'LL INTERVIEW HER EVENTUALLY."

323

IN THE MEANTIME, TAKE THIS DOWN TO SGT. CURSIVE.

THE HANDWRITING EXPERT? WHY THIS IS A RECEIPT FROM **WALTER STRONG**—

SAYING UPPWARD LEE-MOBILE PAID HIM $1,000,000 IN **CASH!**

SOUNDS PRETTY **SUSHI**, HUH? THAT'S HOW US YUPPIES SAY "FISHY."—

YOU GAVE **TRACY** THE PHONY **RECEIPT**?

HE INQUIRED ABOUT STRONG'S FINANCES.

YOU SHOULD HAVE **WAITED!** THEY MIGHT NOT HAVE DISCOVERED ANY DISCREPANCY!

" UPPWARD, SOMETIMES YOUR **THINKING** IS LESS THAN 'STATE OF THE ART.' "

STAKE OUT LEE-MOBILE'S 'TRADING COMPANY'— AND WHEN HE LEAVES, **TAIL** HIM—

HANDWRITING ANALYSIS

SGT. CURSIVE

325

FUMINATING FUTONS, TRENDY! MUST YOU BE SO NEGATIVE?

IF WE ACT LIKE WE'VE NOTHING TO HIDE, TRACY'S SUSPICIONS WILL **DRY UP** LIKE OVERDONE VEAL.

" BESIDES, THAT RECEIPT WAS A **WORLD-CLASS** FAKE. "

THE ✻$#@✻ SIGNATURE APPEARS REAL, BUT...

BUT **WHAT,** SGT. CURSIVE?

3 2 0

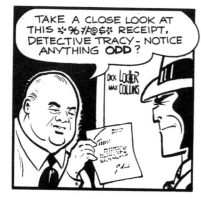

TAKE A CLOSE LOOK AT THIS ✻%#/@$✻ RECEIPT, DETECTIVE TRACY— NOTICE ANYTHING **ODD**?

YES - IT'S **SHAPE**- IT'S SLIGHTLY IRREGULAR- AS IF CUT FROM ANOTHER, LARGER SHEET OF PAPER...

327

"EXACTLY," CURSIVE SAYS. "AN OPINION SUPPORTED BY THE PAPER'S ✻%#$@! WATER MARK BEING CUT IN **HALF**— "

YES, I SAW HER.

© 1986 Tribune Media Services, Inc. All Rights Reserved

COULD STRONG HAVE SIGNED SOME OTHER DOCUMENT - FROM WHICH THIS "NOTE"-SIZE RECEIPT WAS CUT?

DICK LOCHER
MAX COLLINS

AND THESE TYPEWRITTEN LINES **ADDED**?

© 1986 Tribune Media Services, Inc. All Rights Reserved

"$✳#@! YES," SGT. CURSIVE SAYS.

LET'S NOT BICKER - WE CAN WORK ON OUR RELATIONSHIP OVER MESQUITE-GRILLED EELS -

AFTER MY CONDO BOARD MEETING...

© 1986 Tribune Media Services, Inc. All Rights Reserved

HOW'S IT GOING?

THE **GOOD** NEWS IS, SEVERAL JOGGERS **DID** SEE OUR SUSPECT.

THE **BAD** NEWS IS NOBODY RECOGNIZES HER AS A REGULAR.

DICK LOCHER
MAX COLLINS

"THAT'S NOT SO BAD," TRACY SAYS. "IT CONFIRMS OUR SUSPICIONS THAT SHE WAS SPECIFICALLY HERE TO SEE - AND **KILL** - WALTER STRONG."

SO VITAMIN OWNS HIS OWN **MOVIE** THEATER?

YEAH - A REVIVAL HOUSE - PLAYS **CLASSIC** FILMS ONLY.

DID UPPWARD LEE-MOBILE RECOMMEND **THIS** INVESTMENT, VITAMIN?

NO, THIS WAS MY **OWN** NOTION, SAMUEL! THE PUBLIC **CRAVES** CLASSIC CINEMA!

I'VE TURNED NO **FUNDS** OVER TO THEM, AS YET, BUT -

VITAMIN, I BELIEVE THESE PEOPLE MAY BE FRAUDS - AND POSSIBLY INVOLVED IN **MURDER**.

RICHARD, YOUR **FINANCIAL** JUDGEMENT IS OPEN TO QUESTION -

3-30

BUT YOUR INSTINCTS ON MATTERS CRIMINAL ARE ALL BUT **INFALLIBLE**!

WHAT'S HE **TALKING** ABOUT, "RICHARD?"

HE'LL HELP US, SAMUEL.

TAILING UPPWARD LEE-MOBILE HAS **ALREADY** PAID OFF – THE WOMAN HE MET FOR SUPPER...

"MATCHES OUR **SUSPECT** SKETCH OF THE JOGGER SEEN WITH WALTER STRONG."

© 1986 Tribune Media Services, Inc. All Rights Reserved

I'M MEETING VICTOR IN THE PARKING LOT IN FIVE MINUTES, DEAR – TO MAKE A **BUY** –

WONDERFUL! WE'RE RUNNING LOW ON **JAMAICAN**.

44 ®

I'VE TAILED LEE-MOBILE TO A RESTAURANT WHERE HE'S MET A WOMAN WHO'S A **DEAD RINGER** FOR OUR SUSPECT SKETCH!

I OVERHEARD HIM PLANNING TO MEET HIS **CONNECTION** HERE IN THE PARKING LOT –

© 1986 Tribune Media Services, Inc.

"DO WE GO FOR A DRUG BUST?" "YES!" TRACY SAYS.

TIME TO MEET VICTOR.

AND SCORE SOME **JAMAICAN**!

4-5 ®

" I HAD NO IDEA DRUGS WAS LEE-MOBILE'S SCENE," SAM SAYS. "NOR I," ADMITS TRACY "BUT WE'LL TAKE THE BUM **ANY** WAY WE CAN!"

HOW MUCH CAN YOU HANDLE, UPPWARD?

I PROMISED TRENDY I'D SCORE TWO BAGS...

L-BRUCE

FREEZE IT UP, SUCKERS! **POLICE!!** THIS IS A **BUST**!

A BUST...? WHAT'S THE CHARGE?

BURNING BRIOCHE! YOU COPS NEED **THERAPY**!

HAND OVER THE **JAMAICAN**!

CERTAINLY.

© 1986 Tribune Media Services, Inc. All Rights Reserved

BUT SINCE WHEN IS IMPORTED **COFFEE** A CRIME?

® 4-6

219

© 1986 Tribune Media Services, Inc. All Rights Reserved

© 1986 Tribune Media Services, Inc. All Rights Reserved

"CHARLES PONZI WAS A SWINDLER BACK IN THE '20s - HE FLEECED GULLIBLE INVESTORS OF $10 MILLION, PROMISING 100% PROFITS."

WHAT WAS HIS GIMMICK?

HE PAID BACK A FEW EARLY INVESTORS **LAVISHLY** -

YEAH - AND THEY SPREAD THE NEWS, BRINGING IN **LATER** INVESTORS, WHO UNKNOWINGLY HELPED FUND PAYIN' OFF THE **EARLY** INVESTORS

4/13

TRENDY, MR. FLINTHEART HAS A FEW QUESTIONS HE WANTS TO ASK, BEFORE INVESTING.

DICK LOCHER MAX COLLINS

ASK AWAY, MR. FLINTHEART - I THINK YOU'LL FIND US USER FRIENDLY -

4·15 ®

MORE THAN THAT, DEAR, I FIND YOU QUITE CHARMING - AND MIGHT I PERCHANCE SEE A LISTING OF THE BANKS YOU DEAL WITH?

HERE IS AN UP-TO-THE-MINUTE LIST OF BANKS WE'RE ENGAGING IN FOREIGN CURRENCY TRADING -

THE UPPWARD LEE-MOBILE TRADING COMPANY SEEMS AS WELL-CONNECTED AS IT IS ACTIVE!

DICK LOCHER MAX COLLINS

AREN'T YOU RATHER UNDER-STAFFED FOR AN OPERATION OF SUCH MAGNITUDE?

4·16 ®

GRRRR...

HOW CAN YOU SINGLE-HANDEDLY DO ALL THE CURRENCY DEALS IN A MARKET DOMINATED BY 24-HOUR TRADING DESKS?

DICK LOCHER MAX COLLINS

THIS OLD **HAM** KNOWS HIS STUFF -

® 4·17

IT'S QUITE SIMPLE, REALLY.

"I GET IN AND OUT OF THE MARKET QUICKLY, LIQUIDATING NEARLY ALL MY POSITIONS DAILY."

WHERE WE HEADED?

THE MAYOR'S OFFICE -

DIDN'T THE **CHIEF** SAY UPPWARD'S SOCIETY PALS WERE PUTTIN' THE PRESSURE ON TO **LAY OFF** –

THAT'S RIGHT –

OFFICE OF THE MAYOR

Ⓡ 4·18

"BUT WE'RE QUESTIONING HIS TRADING COMPANY'S FANCY CLIENTS, ANYWAY— STARTING WITH **HIS HONOR**— WAIT HERE – "

ONE FINAL QUERY –

WHERE ARE YOUR **BOOKS** AND **RECORDS** KEPT?

©1986 Tribune Media Services, Inc. All Rights Reserved

HOW DID HIS HONOR TAKE TO BEING QUESTIONED?

HE WAS POLITE– LIKE THE CAPTAIN OF A **FIRING SQUAD**.

"HE SAID UPPWARD LEE-MOBILE WAS A FINANCIAL WIZARD AND A PERSONAL **FRIEND**."

©1986 Tribune Media Services, Inc. All Rights Reserved

"WELL," SAM SAYS, "LET'S HOPE VITAMIN ENDS UP WITH A DIFFERENT OUTLOOK – "

I'M **CONVINCED**! I'LL BE INVESTING –

4·19 Ⓡ

MAJOR CRIME SQUAD

I BELIEVE YOUR POLICEMAN'S INTUITION WAS CORRECT M'BOY!

HOW'S THAT, VITAMIN?

YOU WOULDN'T HAPPEN TO BE REFERRIN' TO **UPPWARD LEE-MOBILE**, WOULD YA?

I WOULD INDEED! WHEN I DEIGNED TO QUESTION HIM, REGARDING HIS BUSINESS CONCERNS, HE **ERUPTED** LIKE **VESUVIUS**!

"HIS BETTER HALF HAS A **COOLER**– AND **PRETTIER** HEAD, RICHARD– "

LEE, CALL EVERY BANK ON THIS LIST AND SEE IF THEY'RE REALLY DOING BUSINESS WITH THE LEE-MOBILE TRADING COMPANY.

YOU GOT IT.

222

WITH WHAT LEE DISCOVER-ED WORKIN' FROM VITAMIN'S INFO, WE FINALLY GOT A CASE —

OF FRAUD.

THAT'S JUST FOR OPENERS —HOW 'BOUT **GRAND LARCENY? CONSPIRACY?**

BUT UPPWARD AND TRENDY ARE **MURDERERS—**

4-23

© 1986 Tribune Media Services, Inc. All Rights Reserved

"WE OUGHTA NAIL 'EM FOR **THAT!**"

THE **MAYOR** CALLED TO APOLOGIZE ABOUT THE POLICE **HARASSMENT—**

DICK LOCHER
MAX COLLINS
®

YOU THINK TRACY'S UP TO SOMETHING?

YEAH — HE APOLOGIZED TO UPPWARD!

WE'RE WORKING DAY AND NIGHT PUTTING TOGETHER A CONSPIRACY CASE AGAINST THE LEE-MOBILES, AND TRACY GETS FRIENDLY WITH 'EM?

THAT'S **CRAZY!**

I KNOW! IT'S **NUTS!** THAT'S WHY I FIGURE HE'S PLANNIN' SOME **SOLO** MOVE—

I'M GLAD YOU OPTED TO DROP BY, DETECTIVE TRACY—

THANKS FOR LETTING ME.

4-29

"INTERESTING PLACE YOU HAVE HERE," TRACY SAYS. "WASN'T IT ONCE A **FACTORY?**"

© 1986 Tribune Media Services, Inc. All Rights Reserved

YES, A REAL **SWEATSHOP**, I'M TOLD — NOW IF **YOU'D** CARE TO WORK UP A SWEAT, STEP THIS WAY...

DICK LOCHER
MAX COLLINS
®

QUITE AN IMPRESSIVE LAYOUT- PUTS THE POLICE GYM TO SHAME.

WELCOME TO OUR LIVING SPACE... HEALTH CLUB DEPARTMENT!

WE'RE PLEASED TO ACCOMMODATE YOU, DETECTIVE TRACY.

4-30 ®

© 1986 Tribune Media Services, Inc.
All Rights Reserved

THAT'S "VERY" USER FRIENDLY OF YOU, MS. LEE-MOBILE...

CALL ME **TRENDY.**

DICK LOCHER
MAX COLLINS

© 1986 Tribune Media Services, Inc. All Rights Reserved

WAIT A MINUTE! THESE DOOR HANDLES ARE **SCREWED** ON—

MAYBE IF I COULD **UN**-SCREW THEM, THE HANDLES WOULD **FALL OFF**—

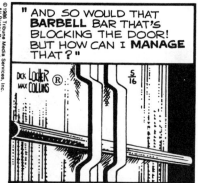

" AND SO WOULD THAT **BARBELL** BAR THAT'S BLOCKING THE DOOR! BUT HOW CAN I **MANAGE** THAT? "

CARELESS CUISINE! WE'VE FORGOTTEN THE DETECTIVE'S 2-WAY WRIST TV! CALM YOURSELF, DEAR—

YOUR LITTLE TRENDY REMOVED THE 'TEC'S HIGH-TECH TOY—

GETTING **WEAK**— BUT THIS MAY **WORK**—

THIS **DIME** MAY SERVE AS A MAKESHIFT **SCREWDRIVER**—

LLOWING ME TO **UNSCREW** THESE DOOR HANDLES—"

IF THIS **HEAT** DOESN'T DO ME IN **FIRST**—

THESE BABIES ARE SCREWED IN **TIGHT**— THIS DIME "SCREW-DRIVER" ISN'T WORTH A **NICKEL**—

BUT IT'S ALL I'VE GOT—

SO I HAVE TO MAKE IT **PAY**—" OUR BEST OPTION? AS WOODY ALLEN ONCE SAID, "TAKE THE MONEY AND RUN"...

THE AUTHORITIES WILL, OF COURSE, BE **SUSPICIOUS** ABOUT DETECTIVE TRACY'S "ACCIDENTAL" DEATH—

BUT BEFORE THAT **AMOUNTS** TO ANYTHING, WE'LL BE **UPPWARDLY MOBILE**—

"**I**NTO THE **SKY**," SAYS TRENDY, "JETTING TO A **NEW LIFE**!"

IT'S **TURNING**!

CRASHING COMMODITIES! IF THAT DETECTIVE HADN'T COME AROUND, OUR TRADING WOULD **STILL** BE **BOOMING**!

IT HAD TO CATCH UP WITH US SOONER OR LATER—CONSIDERING WE **KEPT** ALL THE MONEY OUR CLIENTS GAVE US!

"**T**HAT'S TRUE," UPPWARD SAYS, SETTLING DOWN. "WE NEVER INVESTED A **DIME**!"

THIS **DIME** ISN'T THE **IDEAL** SCREWDRIVER, BUT IT SEEMS TO BE GETTING THE JOB DONE—

THERE!

KLUNK

JUST UNSCREWED **ONE** DOOR HANDLE—THAT'S ALL IT SHOULD TAKE TO...

BUST **OUTA** HERE!

I... I **MADE** IT—

WE'LL DROP THE GREAT DETECTIVE TO THE **BOTTOM** OF THE SHAFT!

DICK LOCHER
MAX COLLINS

"THEN SET THE ELEVATOR DOWN ON HIM — **SQUEEZING** HIM LIKE A GIANT FOOD PROCESSOR!"

ASCENDING

"TRENDY, **PLEASE**," SAYS UPPWARD. "MY DIGESTION!"

© 1986 Tribune Media Services, Inc.
All Rights Reserved

5·31 Ⓡ

TRENDY AND UPPWARD HAVE SENT THE ELEVATOR UP A FLOOR, TO CLEAR THE SHAFT FOR TRACY'S IMMINENT DESCENT —

BUT THEY ARE UNAWARE OF THE PRESENCE, ON THE FLOOR BELOW, OF **SAM CATCHEM** —

WHO HAS PRESSED THE BUTTON BELOW — SUMMONING THE ELEVATOR —

DESCENDING

ON THE COUNT OF THREE, LET'S GIVE HIM THE OLD **HEAVE HO** — ONE.. TWO....

THREE!

BUT TRACY LANDS **UNHARMED** A FEW FEET BELOW, ON THE DESCENDING ELEVATOR —

WHUMP

TRACY! ARE YOU OKAY?

HUH?

DICK LOCHER
MAX COLLINS

DEVASTATING DOWNFALL! THE DETECTIVE IS **SAFE!** WHOOPS.

© 1986 Tribune Media Services, Inc.
All Rights Reserved

UPPWARD?

COULD ONE OF YOU GENTLEMEN GIVE ME A HELPING HAND... THE **SHOCK** OF SEEING MY HUSBAND **FALL** TO HIS DEATH -

® I FEEL **WEAK** - 6-6

UNDERSTANDABLE.

DICK LOCHER MAX COLLINS

SAM! WATCH OUT - HER **FINGERNAIL**...

THANKS, TRENDY- YOU'VE JUST MADE OUR CASE A LITTLE **STRONGER** -

UNLESS I MISS MY **GUESS**, THIS IS ONE **LETHAL** FINGERNAIL... THE "POLISH" IS STILL **WET** -

© 1986 Tribune Media Services, Inc. All Rights Reserved

WE'LL CLIP IT AT THE STATION, AS EVIDENCE - IN THE MEANTIME, TRY NOT TO **SCRATCH** YOURSELF -

6/7 ®

DICK LOCHER MAX COLLINS

THOUGHT YOU'D LIKE TO KNOW THE **UPPWARD LEE-MOBILE** CASE HAS BEEN SUCCESSFULLY SOLVED - THANKS IN PART TO **YOU** -

"UPPWARD FELL TO HIS DEATH IN AN ELEVATOR SHAFT, AND TRENDY IS BEHIND BARS - "

AN ELEVATOR SHAFT, EH? WELL WHAT GOES **UP** -

WE THINK MUCH OF THE MONEY THEY STOLE WILL BE RECOVERED.

6 8 ®

EGAD! I NEARLY GAVE THOSE BRIGANDS MY **TREASURE**! RICHARD, YOUR ADVICE HAS ONCE AGAIN PROVED **SOUND** -

WHAT **WOULD** YOU SUGGEST I INVEST MY MONEY IN?

YOU COULD START WITH A TICKET TO THE POLICEMAN'S BALL.

WHAT WAS THEIR FATAL **MISTAKE,** SAMUEL?

THAT'S EASY- THEY SHOULDN'TA GOT DICK TRACY **STEAMED** -

6-9 ®

Dick Tracy Goes to Hollywood

ACTION, in capital letters, has always been a keystone of Chester Gould's Dick Tracy. This factor and the comic strip's incredible popularity, especially with young boys, led Republic Pictures to feature Dick Tracy in four Saturday afternoon serials between 1937 and 1941.

In just six years, Chester Gould's creation had made the jump from newsprint to film and further widened the audience and influence of America's most famous detective.

Besides Dick Tracy, Republic featured other comic strip characters in its serials. These included Red Ryder, King of the Royal Mounties, Captain Marvel, Spy Smasher, and Captain America. However, only Dick Tracy was featured in four action-packed serials, each 15 episodes long.

For actor Ralph Byrd, the year 1937 was pivotal in his career. Nat Levine, owner of Republic Pictures, signed him to play Dick Tracy in the first Tracy serial and placed him under contract to Republic. It was a role that Byrd would portray on and off until his untimely death from a heart attack in 1952. Byrd's acceptance as the screen's Dick Tracy rivals that of Clayton Moore as The Lone Ranger and George Reeves as Superman.

Byrd was born in Dayton, Ohio, in 1909. He'd toured the Middle West with theatrical groups and sung on radio before he came west to study at the Hollywood Little Theatre. There he was spotted by a Columbia Pictures talent scout and signed to appear

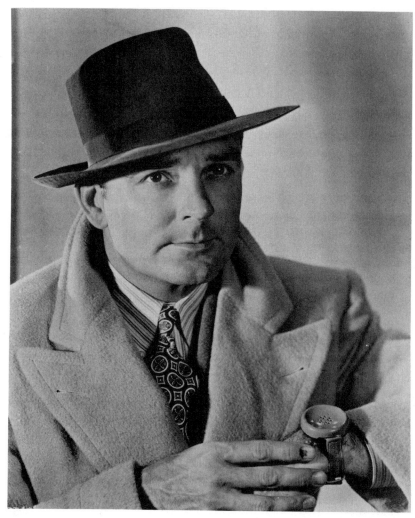

Ralph Byrd tunes in his two-way wrist radio. The actor's portrayal of Dick Tracy in movie matinee serials, in feature films and on television was the apex of his career.

The posters for Dick Tracy serials featured action and Chester Gould art.

in *Hell Ship Morgan* (Columbia 1936).

In 1937, Byrd not only starred in *Dick Tracy* for Republic, but also starred in the 15-episode serial *Blake of Scotland Yard*, released by Victory Pictures.

Dick Tracy, as a serial film, did not debut unchallenged. Just as they were rivals on the comic pages, the Tribune Syndicate's Dick Tracy met his competition, King Feature's Secret Agent X-9, played by Scott Kolk, on the silver screen. Secret Agent X-9 was created by Dashiell Hammett and in the comics drawn by Alex Raymond, the artist who made Flash Gordon a science-fiction superstar. However, today, only Dick Tracy remains a superstar of the comic page.

A measure of Dick Tracy's popularity was that at Republic Pictures the favored length of serials was 12 episodes. However, all of the Tracy serials had 15 episodes. By contrast, 43 of Republic's 66 serials fell into the 12-episode category.

Serials were aimed at the youthful Saturday matinee audience and were not designed to faithfully represent the mythology of a comic strip character for character. For example, Republic Pictures changed Dick Tracy from a policeman to a G-man. Also Tess Trueheart, Tracy's long-time fiancée, is missing. She's replaced with a girlfriend named Gwen.

However, the Tracy serials had the good fortune to have some of the best talent in movie serials working on them.

Dick Tracy (1937) starred Ralph Byrd in his first role as "G-man" Tracy. Kay Hughes played Gwen. The serial was filmed long before Tracy's sidekick Sam Catchem made his first appearance in 1948. At this time Pat Patton, who later became chief of police, is Tracy's partner. However, he was dropped by Republic in favor of a stooge character, Mike McGurk, played by Gene Autry's longtime sidekick Smiley Burnette.

Key to the success of the first serial was the Republic studios' fine model and special effects department headed by the brothers Howard and Theodore Lydecker. While the competition relied on cheaply made table-top miniatures, the Lydeckers were allowed to use large-scale, superbly crafted models. These in turn were pho-

tographed outside against natural skies. In *Dick Tracy*, the main villain is The Spider, whose identity remains a secret until the last episode. The Spider's futuristic airplane, The Flying Wing, is so powerful it can destroy a suspension bridge. In fact, the model for The Flying Wing made by the Lydeckers was so good that Republic used it again in 1938 as The Lightning for *The Fighting Devil Dogs*.

Besides Dick Tracy himself, only Junior Tracy, played by Lee Van Atta, remained a character true to the comic strip. The film had wonderful action sequences and Ray Taylor and Alan James, both veteran directors, share the credits. It was quite normal for two directors to be used in the filming of serials. Customarily one handled the dialogue scenes and fights, while the other took care of large action scenes.

The success of *Dick Tracy* brought the second 15-episode series, *Dick Tracy Returns*, to movie audiences in 1938. Only Ralph Byrd as Tracy remained among the

Morgan Conway, selected by RKO to portray Dick Tracy in his full-length feature film debut in 1945, receives some tips from tracy's creator Chester Gould. The cover of the book Conway is studying shows the type of stunning, highly designed ar twork that usually accompanied Dick Tracy licensed items.

principals. Jerry Tucker now played Junior Tracy, and Lee Ford was now Mike McGurk, the comic relief. Lynne Roberts played Tracy's girlfriend, Gwen.

Dick Tracy Returns and the remaining two serials, *Dick Tracy's G-Men* (1939) and *Dick Tracy vs. Crime, Inc.* (1941), were all directed by one of the most dynamic teams of action-directors in the heyday of serial movies, William Whitney and John English.

The villain in *Dick Tracy Returns* is Stark, played by Charles Middleton, who heads the Stark gang comprised of his five extremely reprehensible sons. They are, however, no match for Dick Tracy.

The third serial, *Dick Tracy's G-Men* (1939), benefited not only from the direction of Whitney and English and a fine performance by Byrd, but had a memorable original musical score by William Lava. Republic Pictures was the only studio to use original musical scores for their serials. Lava later worked at RKO and Warner Brothers.

Irving Pichel played the villain Zarnon in this third serial. Pichel was also a director whose credits included the 1935 RKO film *She,* based on the H. Rider Haggard novel. While both Junior and Mike "stooge" McGurk are missing from *Dick Tracy's G-Men,* the serial marks an early film appearance of Jennifer Jones as the girlfriend, Gwen.

However, by the fourth and last serial, *Dick Tracy vs. Crime, Inc.* (1941), Gwen has been cut and replaced by a new girlfriend for Tracy, June Chandler, portrayed by actress Jan Wiley. This final serial featured the villain, The Ghost, who true to his name had the ability of becoming invisible. While the plot had little similarity to anything Chester Gould might have presented in his comic strip, it was fun, action-packed and well received by Saturday matinee audiences in pre-World War II America.

Hollywood's interest in Tracy lay dormant during the World War II years, a time when the momentum of the comic strip was building with the introduction of the arch-villains Pruneface and his wife, Flattop, The Brow, Shakey, Gravel Gertie, Vitamin Flintheart, B.O. Plenty and Breathless Mahoney. Gould's penchant for weird and bizarre villains was taking off. The popularity of Dick Tracy soared.

The next appearance of Tracy on the big screen was a feature film produced by RKO in 1945. William Berke directed in a style known as *film noir* (literally "black film").

The term was first used by French film critics in the 1950s to describe American crime and gangster movies of the 1930s and '40s. *Film noir* emphasized moody lighting, strong contrast between light and shadow, a sense of foreboding, a dark view of life, and a sense of fatality. Many of these sensations had been fixtures in Chester Gould's work for years. *Dick Tracy* the film and Dick Tracy the character were made for each other.

For the film RKO cast Morgan Conway in the lead role. Tracy is once again a policeman, not a G-man, as in the serials. Conway had a different style than Byrd but made a very credible Dick Tracy. Anne Jeffreys played Tess Trueheart, who finally made the silver screen. Lyle Latell played Pat Patton and Mickey Kuhn was Junior Tracy.

Splitface, a vicious slasher, was por-

Gagged and bound, Tess Trueheart (right), portrayed by Anne Jeffreys, and a friend are at the dubious mercy of deranged slasher Splitface portrayed by Mike Mazurki in *Dick Tracy*, the first RKO film with Gould's hero.

DICK TRACY

Dick Tracy's ROGUES' GALLERY

GRUESOME–
BANK ROBBER WHO RUTHLESSLY MURDERED ACCOMPLICES. SERVING LIFE. *(AS PORTRAYED by BORIS KARLOFF IN RKO FILM DICK TRACY MEETS GRUESOME, 1947.)*

2-WAY WRIST TV

Dick Tracy's ROGUES' GALLERY

SPLITFACE–
KNIFE-WIELDING MURDERER WHO ESCAPED PRISON and BEGAN MURDERING JURORS WHO CONVICTED HIM. SERVING LIFE. *(PORTRAYED by MIKE MAZURKI in RKO FILM, DICK TRACY, 1945.)*

Dick Tracy's ROGUES' GALLERY

CUEBALL–
JEWEL THIEF; MURDERER. STRANGLED VICTIMS with LEATHER HATBAND. STRUCK AND KILLED BY TRAIN ATTEMPTING TO ELUDE POLICE. *(PORTRAYED by DICK WESSEL IN RKO FILM DICK TRACY vs. CUEBALL, 1946.)*

GOULD
Fletcher
COLLINS

DICK TRACY on FILM

1930s – REPUBLIC SERIALS STARRING RALPH BYRD.

1940s – RKO FEATURES STARRING MORGAN CONWAY, THEN BYRD.

1950s – ABC-TV SERIES STARRING BYRD.

1960s – UPA CARTOON SERIES, SYNDICATED, FILMATION CARTOON SERIES.

1970s – PARAMOUNT ANNOUNCES 1978 FILM PRODUCTION.

© 1978 by The Chicago Tribune
All Rights Reserved

Cueball (Dick Wessel, the skin-domed hitman of a jewel heist gang, attempts to strangle Tess Trueheart (Anne Jeffreys), but Dick Tracy (Morgan Conway) initiates a change of plan for the would-be killer in this publicity photo from *Dick Tracy vs. Cueball* (RKO, 1946).

trayed by Mike Mazurki with a horrible scar across his cheek. The plot has Split-face brutally removing the members of a jury that had previously convicted him.

Chester Gould, ever the master of publicity, was delighted to review the film for his hometown paper, the Chicago *Tribune.*

"The gentleman with whom I had shared sweat, blood and tears for almost 15 years," he wrote, "Dick Tracy in the flesh, Morgan Conway's flesh, to be exact, right on the screen at the Palace. And for once he did the talking and I listened. I felt pretty helpless, too, because I couldn't use a piece of art gum to change his face or hat, and what he said came from a script and not from a stubby old lead pencil held by yours truly."

The script was a well-written one by Eric Taylor, a veteran of most of the Columbia Pictures detective movies. The film was later renamed *Dick Tracy, Detective.*

Morgan Conway also starred in *Dick Tracy vs. Cueball* (RKO, 1946). Cueball, portrayed by Dick Wessel, was the bald-headed hitman for a trio of jewel theives. He strangles three victims before his pursuit by Dick Tracy. The chase, a classic Gould technique, takes Tracy and Cueball to a railroad yard where Cueball gets a permanent kiss from a locomotive. Anne Jeffreys again portrayed Tess Trueheart. Ian Keith played Vitamin Flintheart and looked as if he had stepped off Gould's comics page.

With *Dick Tracy vs. Cueball*, RKO made an effort to capture the spirit of the comic strip. The screenplay was by Dane Lussier and Robert E. Kent.

After this second Dick Tracy feature film, Morgan Conway's option was not renewed by RKO. Instead, the studio hired Ralph Byrd, whose characterization of Tracy had been honed in the Republic serials. Also, Kay Christopher replaced Anne Jeffreys as Tess Trueheart.

Dick Tracy's Dilemma (RKO, 1947) features a gang of crooks headed by The Claw, a thug whose right hand has been replaced with a steel hook. Jack Lambert portrayed The Claw. The gang murders a night watchman during a fur heist. It's Dick Tracy's job to bring them and their well-placed mastermind to justice. In the best Gould tradition, The Claw proves to be just a flash in the pan when confronted by Tracy. He's electrocuted when his steel claw becomes entangled in a live trolley wire.

The final Dick Tracy feature film, to date, was *Dick Tracy Meets Gruesome* (RKO, 1947). It is also the least satisfying. It is hard to believe that the same Eric Taylor, involved in so many fine mysteries, participated in the scripting. The film was based on a drug the criminals use that temporarily freezes people in place, allowing the crooks to rob banks. Byrd again played Tracy.

However, if the plot was a bit farfetched, past what Gould might himself have thought up, parts of the dialogue are embarrassing. Boris Karloff played Gruesome in a professional if uninspired manner. Needless to say, Tracy triumphs. However, the bottom line and need for economy at RKO succeeded in doing what neither Split-face, Cueball, The Claw, or Gruesome could. They removed Dick Tracy from the silver screen.

The character Vitamin Flintheart virtually jumps from the comic page to life in the person of actor Ian Keith in a remarkable mekeup job. Morgan Conway as Tracy and Anne Jeffreys as Tess Trueheart complete the trio in this scene from *Dick Tracy vs. Cueball* (RKOS, 1946).

Meanwhile, Dick Tracy the comic strip had not even yet peaked in popularity. America took to heart the wedding of B.O. Plenty and Gravel Gertie. Their daughter, Sparkle Plenty, created a sensation and the Sparkle Plenty doll was a huge hit.

It seems proper that Dick Tracy, a comic strip so associated with being in the forefront of new developments, should be rescued by television.

Ralph Byrd, *the* Dick Tracy of the screen, was signed to portray Tracy in 39 half-hour television stories. The production of 26 episodes began in November 1949. Angela Greene portrayed Tess Trueheart and Joe Devlin played Sam Catchem, who had been missing from all previous Tracy films. The show aired on the ABC network in prime-time from September 11, 1950, until February 12, 1951. Then from February 17, 1951, until March 31, 1951, it aired on Saturdays. Following that "Dick Tracy," the TV show, went into syndication.

The year 1951 was an important one for the fledgeling television industry. It was the first year commercial television crossed over into becoming a profit-producing business. That year there were about 7,500,000 TV sets in America, and the 108 TV stations in 63 cities permitted by the Federal Communications Commission were already doing about half the dollar volume in sales of the 2,000 radio stations in some 1,200 markets.

Dick Tracy on television, as you might expect, was caught up in the 1954 Senate Committee hearing on juvenile delinquency. The violence in the show was de-

With his fedora knocked askew, Dick Tracy (Ralph Byrd) finds himself in a tough spot in his last feature film *Dick Tracy Meets Gruesome* (RKO, 1947). Boris Karloff as Gruesome and Skelton Knaggs as his accomplice mistakenly assume that they will finish off America's most famous detective.

nounced from some quarters and it was cited along with Captain Midnight and Captain Video and his Video Rangers as being dubious entertainment for children.

Tracy's last appearance on television was as a five-minute cartoon series done in embarrassingly limited animation. UPA produced the Saturday morning show in 1961. Tracy is joined by such un-Gouldian helpers as Hemlock Holmes, Heap O'Calories, Joe Jitsu, and the Retouchables. Everett Sloane did Tracy's voice. Veterans Mel Blanc and Paul Frees provided the other voices. Unbelievably, the animated Tracy was rerun in 1971 on "Archie's TV Funnies."

Happily, Dick Tracy's career on the screen did not end with the ignominity of limited animation. After the option on a Dick Tracy film floated around Hollywood for nine years at $150,000 per year, a movie has been co-produced by Warren Beatty and the Walt Disney Co.

Dick Tracy, directed by Beatty who also stars in the title role, debuts in June 1990. Madonna adds sizzle to the film as sexy Breathless Mahoney.

Drawing of Jack Lambert as "The Claw," the villain in the RKO film *Dick Tracy's Dilemma*, used as part of the Rogues' Gallery mini-feature on a Collins-Fletcher Sunday page.

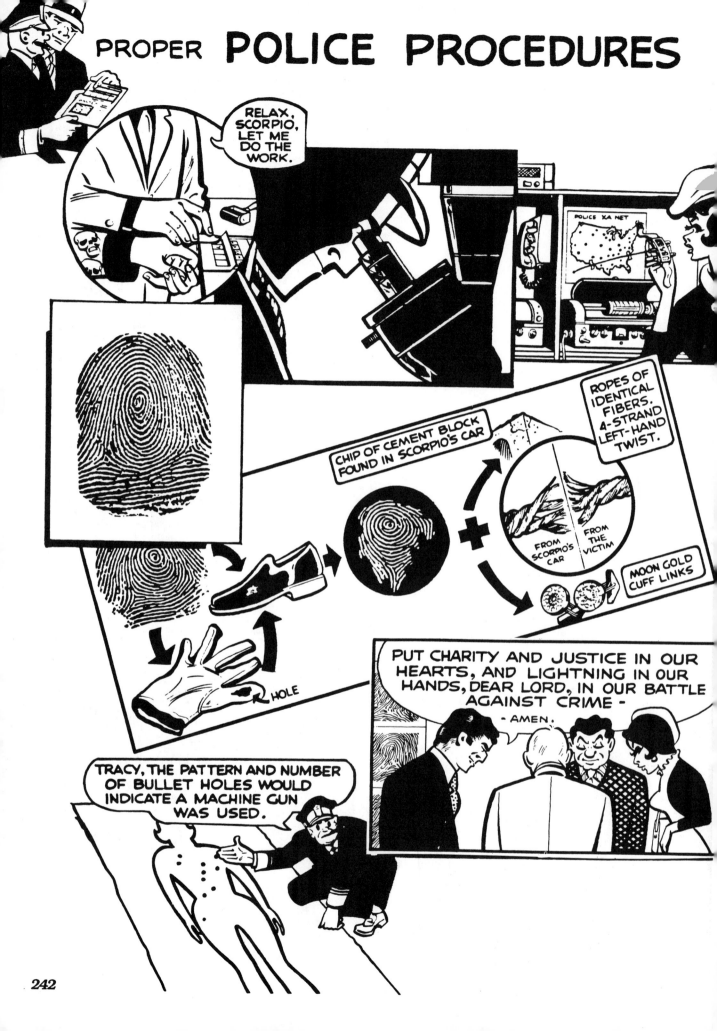

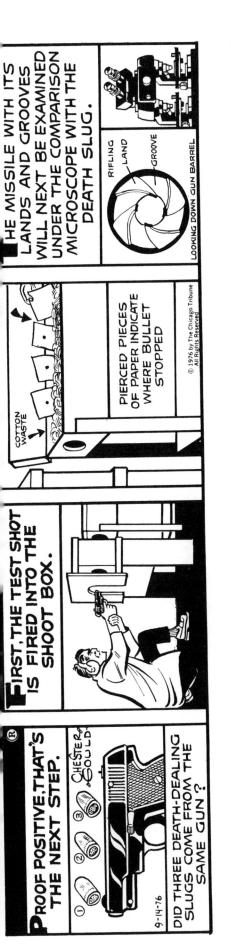

THE MISSILE WITH ITS LANDS AND GROOVES WILL NEXT BE EXAMINED UNDER THE COMPARISON MICROSCOPE WITH THE DEATH SLUG.

RIFLING
LAND
GROOVE

LOOKING DOWN GUN BARREL

COTTON WASTE

PIERCED PIECES OF PAPER INDICATE WHERE BULLET STOPPED

© 1976 by The Chicago Tribune All Rights Reserved

FIRST, THE TEST SHOT IS FIRED INTO THE SHOOT BOX.

PROOF POSITIVE, THAT'S THE NEXT STEP.

CHESTER GOULD

① ② ③

DID THREE DEATH-DEALING SLUGS COME FROM THE SAME GUN?

9-14-76

AND FINALLY THE COMPARISON MICROSCOPE—

MATCHED

NON-MATCHING

FIRING PINS LEAVE THEIR OWN DISTINCTIVE MARKS ON FIRING CAPS

INCRIMINATING SAME MARK BY SUSPECT WEAPON

®

BUT NOT SO WITH BULLETS FROM AN AUTOMATIC WHICH HAVE OUTER COVERINGS OF NICKELED ALLOY.

ALLOY JACKET

LEAD CORE

EJECTOR MARKS FOR COMPARISON

9-15-76

CHESTER GOULD

LEAD BULLETS SOMETIMES CARRY IMPRINTS OF THE FABRIC THE VICTIM WAS WEARING—

NOSE ENLARGED

.38

© 1976 by The Chicago Tribune All Rights Reserved

© 1976 by The Chicago Tribune
All Rights Reserved

FATAL SLUGS

'JUKE-JOY' TEST BULLET

3 MATCHES!

YES, CHIEF, THE LAST FIVE YEARS IT SEEMS BOLO AND BIG CHARLEY HAVE PLAYED A LOT OF MUSIC WITH A .32 AUTOMATIC.

CHESTER GOULD

THREE FATAL SLUGS

CASE #1160 4/12/76

AND SO THE GUN THAT WAS FOUND IN A VINYL "BISCUIT" IN THE "JUKE JOY" RECORDING STUDIO ACCOUNTS FOR THREE MURDERS.

9-16-76

Tracy's High-tech Arsenal

Space Coupe (1962-1978)

Air-Car (1964-1977)

ce-O-Graf (1968)

cal Network Receiver for 2-Way Wrist TV

ser Gun with camera (1964-1977)

Origins of the Wrist Radio

Dick Tracy's trademark two-way wrist radio first appeared on Sunday, January 13, 1946, in the unlikely hands of B.O. Plenty.

Still a fugitive from the law, B.O. had taken a job as a groundsman at industrialist Diet Smith's mansion. The wrist radio had been dropped by a man who bumped into him.

Simultaneously Diet Smith's business partner for the past 30 years had been murdered and Diet was the prime suspect.

By Saturday, January 19, 1946, Dick Tracy had studied the radio and come to the conclusion, "I think he has uncovered the most remarkable invention of the age."

The dual mysteries took Chester Gould many weeks to unravel.

The actual inventor of the two-way wrist radio was Brilliant, a young blind genius of a scientist, whose only goal was bettering man's lot.

"Even though my experiments have blinded me, I shall continue my research together," says Brilliant. "Mother and I shall serve humanity."

However, for Brilliant's mother, Irma, charity and concern for humanity goes no further than her own pocketbook. She dreams of riches from her son's discovery and plans to manufacture the radio herself. Irma, a 20-year employee with Diet Smith Industries, decides the best way to manufacture the radio is to steal parts from the factory.

Her husband attempts the heist and is killed for his troubles. Irma in grief and rage breaks into Diet Smith's home bent on revenge. But when she confronts Smith she ends up turning her weapon on herself and commits suicide.

It is at this point that young Brilliant joins Diet Smith Industries as the star inventor. One would think that the inventor of the two-way wrist radio would have a bright future after all his suffering in the past. That was not what Chester Gould planned for Brilliant.

Two years later (1948), the young scientist is murdered by criminals attempting to secure the plans for the two-way wrist radio for themselves. Only then does Diet Smith reveal to Dick Tracy that in fact

Brilliant was his son. Years ago Diet had been involved in a brief marriage with Irma that had produced Brilliant.

Chester Gould says that he actually thought up the concept of a two-way wrist television at the same time he conjured up the two-way wrist radio. However, he felt that would have been so far out in 1946 that few readers would think it even possible. By contrast, most people knew of the walkie-talkies used in World War II, and the radio idea worked.

The radio was powered by a tiny atomic battery. The early radio had a range of 500 miles for two-way operation. Then on June 23, 1956, in the middle of the Flattop, Jr., story, Gould had Diet Smith visit Tracy and Sam with an updated version a few months after the 10th anniversary of the wrist radio.

The major improvement was an increase in two-way range to cover 2,500 miles. A Sunday page in 1954 had mentioned a range of 1,000 miles so this was the second improvement over the original 500-mile range.

Gould's desire to be a step ahead and his interest in the space program led him to have Diet Smith develop the magnetic space coupe, a space ship powered by the earth's magnetism, in August 1962. This ushers in the sometimes controversial Gould "space" period, which he denied was ever science-fiction.

"Although I'm not a prophet, I do believe that that will happen. It [magnetic propulsion] will do away with all this fire and brimstone that accompanies a rocket's taking off today." said Chester Gould. "I still think that getting around the universe will be a simple thing someday."

Simple or not, Gould's interest in space and the moon dominated the storyline of the strip for several years. It brought so many new inventions to the strip that were so far in the future that the change from two-way wrist radio to two-way wrist television was almost overshadowed.

However, by spring 1964 when the two-way wrist TV first appeared, America had changed from what it was in January 1946. Television, the one-eyed monster, the boob tube, the idiot box, the king of enter-

tainment had become a fixture in Americans' home and lifestyles. The amazing thing about the wrist TV was that it was two-way. Chester Gould used this device with dramatic effect in the strip.

Technology changes daily and by 1984, in a story written by Max Allan Collins to honor George Orwell's novel by the same name, the villain is supplying street vendors of fake designer jeans and shirts with two-way wrist radios to avoid the police.

"Tracy makes the comment in that strip that the police are paying the same price in the technological society as everyone else— loss of privacy," says Collins. Granted in terms of the strip the crooks were using 38-year-old technology, but still they had access to it.

Actually, in the story by Collins the plot is considerably more sinister. Big Brother Co., an organized crime operation, has unscrambled the police's video signals and is making them available for a price on an underworld cable TV network.

The final variation of the two-way wrist radio was introduced into the strip in June 1986, the two-way wrist computer.

The computer developed as the result of a brainstorming session in Chicago in January 1986 between writer Max Allan Collins, artist Dick Locher, and Tribune Media Services editor Mike Argirion. Their goal, at which they succeeded, was to keep America's most famous detective a step ahead in wrist communications and technology.

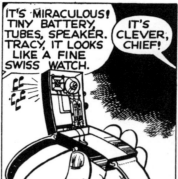

The Origin of the Two-Way Wrist TV

I CHASED HIM AWAY AS SURELY AS THOUGH I HAD USED A CLUB.

ARE WE STILL RUNNING A POLICE DEPARTMENT AROUND HERE OR IS THIS THE OLD PEOPLE'S HOME?

TRACY, I HAVE SOMETHING TO SHOW YOU.

DID YOU EVER SEE A 2-WAY WRIST TELEVISION?

A 2-WAY WRIST TELEVISION!

IT OPENS UP A WHOLE NEW WORLD IN CRIME DETECTION WORK!

YOU CAN TELEVISE THE SCENE NOW AS WELL AS DESCRIBE IT.

HOW DO I LOOK, STUDENTS? HOW DO I LOOK?

THE HAM'S BEST FRIEND!

DICK TRACY

CRIMESTOPPERS TEXTBOOK

WARNING! ACCEPTING A RIDE WITH STRANGERS IN A BOAT CAN BE EVEN MORE DANGEROUS THAN ACCEPTING A RIDE IN A CAR. *Dick Tracy*

YES, I SEE SAM—AND I HEAR YOU CLEARLY, MACK.

THE FIRST AND ONLY 2-WAY WRIST TELEVISION IN THE WORLD! DIET SMITH'S NEWEST CONTRIBUTION TO THE FIGHT AGAINST CRIME!

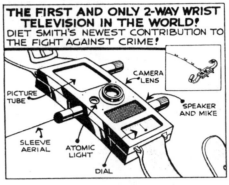

WE'RE TALKING TO YOU FROM THE POLICE GARAGE AT WOOD AVENUE. WE'RE OVER 12 MILES AWAY.

THE RANGE HAS NOT YET BEEN ESTABLISHED, BUT WE BELIEVE IT TO BE NEARLY LIMITLESS.

A NEW AND MORE POWERFUL ATOMIC BULLET FEEDS THE POWER TO THE SMALLEST TV CAMERA EVER BUILT.

"A SPECIAL LENS GIVES A 180° VIEW WHEN NEEDED, AND IT CAN BE SECRETLY PLACED IN A ROOM FOR SURVEILLANCE PURPOSES."

—"OR HID IN A CAR."

"IT HAS ITS OWN ATOMIC LIGHT FOR VIEWING INACCESSIBLE, UNLIGHTED PLACES, AND—"

TRACY—YOU DON'T SEEM ENTHUSED. AREN'T YOU EXCITED?

OH, I'M EXCITED

BUT I'M GETTING OUT OF THIS BUSINESS—THAT'S ALL —GETTING OUT.

YOU'RE GETTING OUT?

YEAH, I'M GETTING OUT. OUT, **OUT!** YOU HEARD ME—OUT!

SINCE JUNIOR DISAPPEARED WITH MOON MAID, TRACY'S COMPLETELY CHANGED, HE'S DYING BY INCHES.

The Origin of the Two-Way Wrist Computer

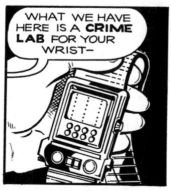

THE 2-WAY WRIST COMPUTER IS **USELESS** TO ANYONE BUT ITS **PROPER WEARER**—

HOW SO?

6·17 R

AS YOU KNOW, **HEARTBEAT PATTERNS** ARE AS INDIVIDUAL AS **FINGERPRINTS**—

DICK LODER MAX COLLINS

© 1986 Tribune Media Services, Inc. All Rights Reserved

THAT LITTLE DEVICE IS PROGRAMMED TO MONITOR AND RECOGNIZE **YOUR HEARTBEAT**—

BECAUSE THE 2-WAY WRIST COMPUTER IS TIED TO YOUR HEARTBEAT, IT CAN SEND A **WARNING SIGNAL** TO HQ—

R 6/18

SHOULD MY HEART-BEAT BECOME **IRREGULAR**, YOU MEAN—OR STOP ALTOGETHER.

DICK LODER MAX COLLINS

© 1986 Tribune Media Services, Inc. All Rights Reserved

YES—AND HQ WILL BE ABLE TO TRACK YOUR LOCATION—YOU'RE WEARING A **HOMING DEVICE**—"

OFFICER DOWN—

THIS IS AN INCREDIBLE DEVICE, DIET—BUT HOW IS IT A **"CRIME LAB"** FOR MY WRIST?

R 6·19

THIS TINY **STEEL PROBE** ALLOWS FOR ON-THE-SPOT **CHEMICAL ANALYSIS**—

© 1986 Tribune Media Services, Inc. All Rights Reserved

DICK LODER MAX COLLINS

IT WILL TELL YOU THE COMPARISON OF SOIL-BLOOD TYPE i.e.— TOXICITY OF CHEMICALS- OH, AND THE TIME OF DAY...

YOUR FLAT **LCD*** SCREEN PROVIDES FOUR LINES OF DATA—

R DICK LODER MAX COLLINS

*****LIQUID CRYSTAL DISPLAY**

AND STILL FUNCTIONS AS A 2-WAY TV SCREEN—

TRACY—

© 1986 Tribune Media Services, Inc. All Rights Reserved

SO I NOTICE," TRACY SAYS. "THE CHIEF HAS JUST ORDERED ME BACK TO HQ—I'M WANTED IN **WASHINGTON, D.C.**—"

6·20